Cook Memorial Public Library

3 1122 01599 1701

APR 1 4 2021

P9-CQW-201

NATAN SHARANSKY

FREEDOM FIGHTER FOR SOVIET JEWS

Blake Hoena ✶ Daniele Dickmann

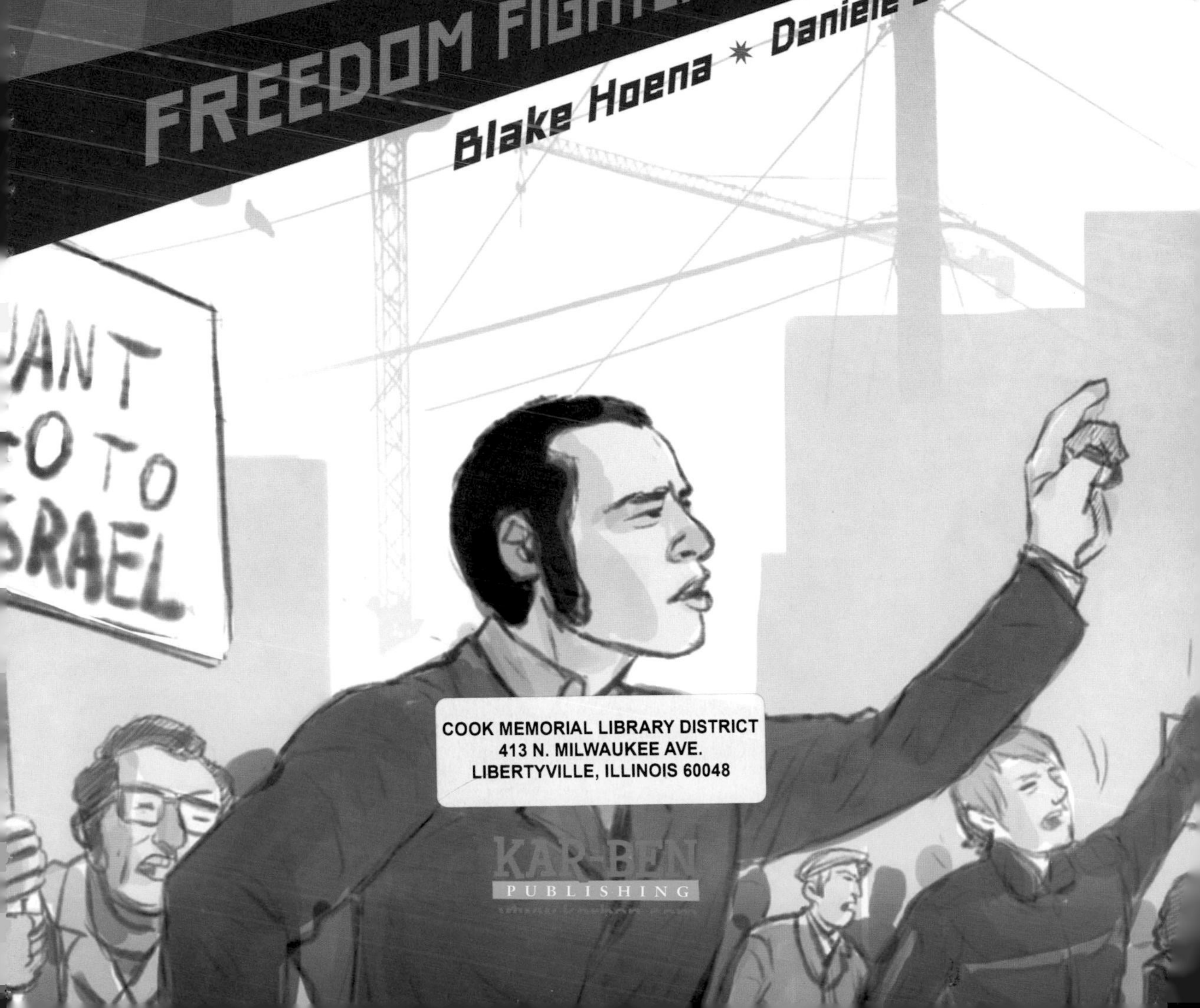

KAR-BEN
PUBLISHING

Copyright © 2021 by Lerner Publishing Group, Inc.

All rights reserved. International copyright secured. No part of this book may be reproduced, stored in a retrieval system, or transmitted in any form or by any means—electronic, mechanical, photocopying, recording, or otherwise—without the prior written permission of Lerner Publishing Group, Inc., except for the inclusion of brief quotations in an acknowledged review.

KAR-BEN PUBLISHING®
An imprint of Lerner Publishing Group, Inc.
241 First Avenue North
Minneapolis, MN 55401 USA
Website address: www.karben.com

Photo Acknowledgments
Photos on page 62 are courtesy of: Harry Lerner (top); Yaakov Saar/Israel National Photo Collection (middle); Amos Ben Gershom/Israel National Photo Collection (bottom).

Main body text set in Comicrazy.
Typeface provided by Comicraft.

Library of Congress Cataloging-in-Publication Data

Names: Hoena, B. A., author. | Dickmann, Daniele, illustrator.
Title: Natan Sharansky : freedom fighter for Soviet Jews / Blake Hoena ; illustrated by Daniele Dickmann.
Description: Minneapolis, MN : Kar-Ben Publishing , [2021] | Includes bibliographical references. | Audience: Ages 8–11 | Audience: Grades 4–6 | Summary: "The story of Soviet Jewry refusenik and human rights activist Anatoly Natan Sharansky"— Provided by publisher.
Identifiers: LCCN 2020016337 (print) | LCCN 2020016338 (ebook) | ISBN 9781541588998 (library binding) | ISBN 9781728404684 (paperback) | ISBN 9781728417561 (ebook)
Subjects: LCSH: Graphic novels. | CYAC: Graphic novels. | Shcharansky, Anatoly—Fiction. | Jews—Soviet Union—Biography—Fiction.
Classification: LCC PZ7.7.H64 Nat 2021 (print) | LCC PZ7.7.H64 (ebook) | DDC 741.5/973—dc23

LC record available at https://lccn.loc.gov/2020016337
LC ebook record available at https://lccn.loc.gov/2020016338

Manufactured in the United States of America
1-47461-48026-7/30/2020

TABLE OF CONTENTS

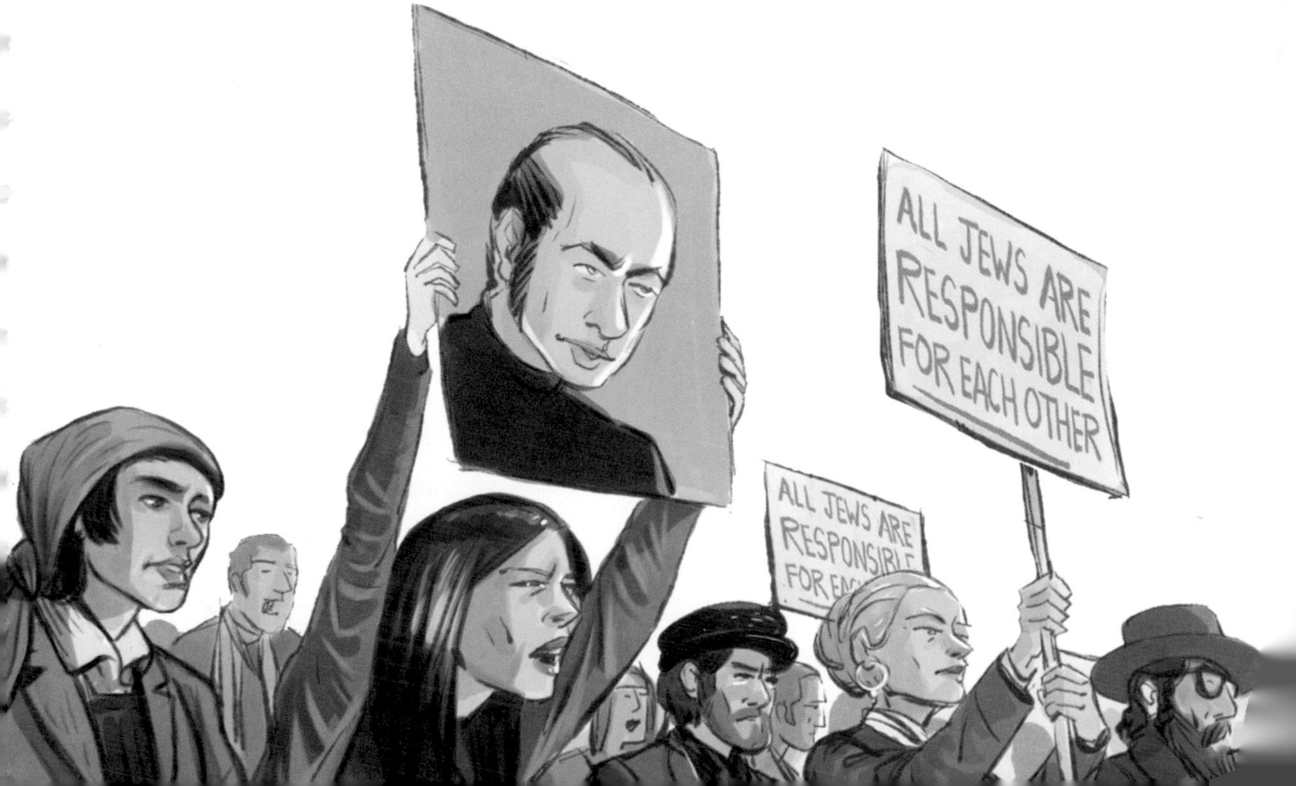
ALL JEWS ARE RESPONSIBLE FOR EACH OTHER
ALL JEWS ARE RESPONSIBLE

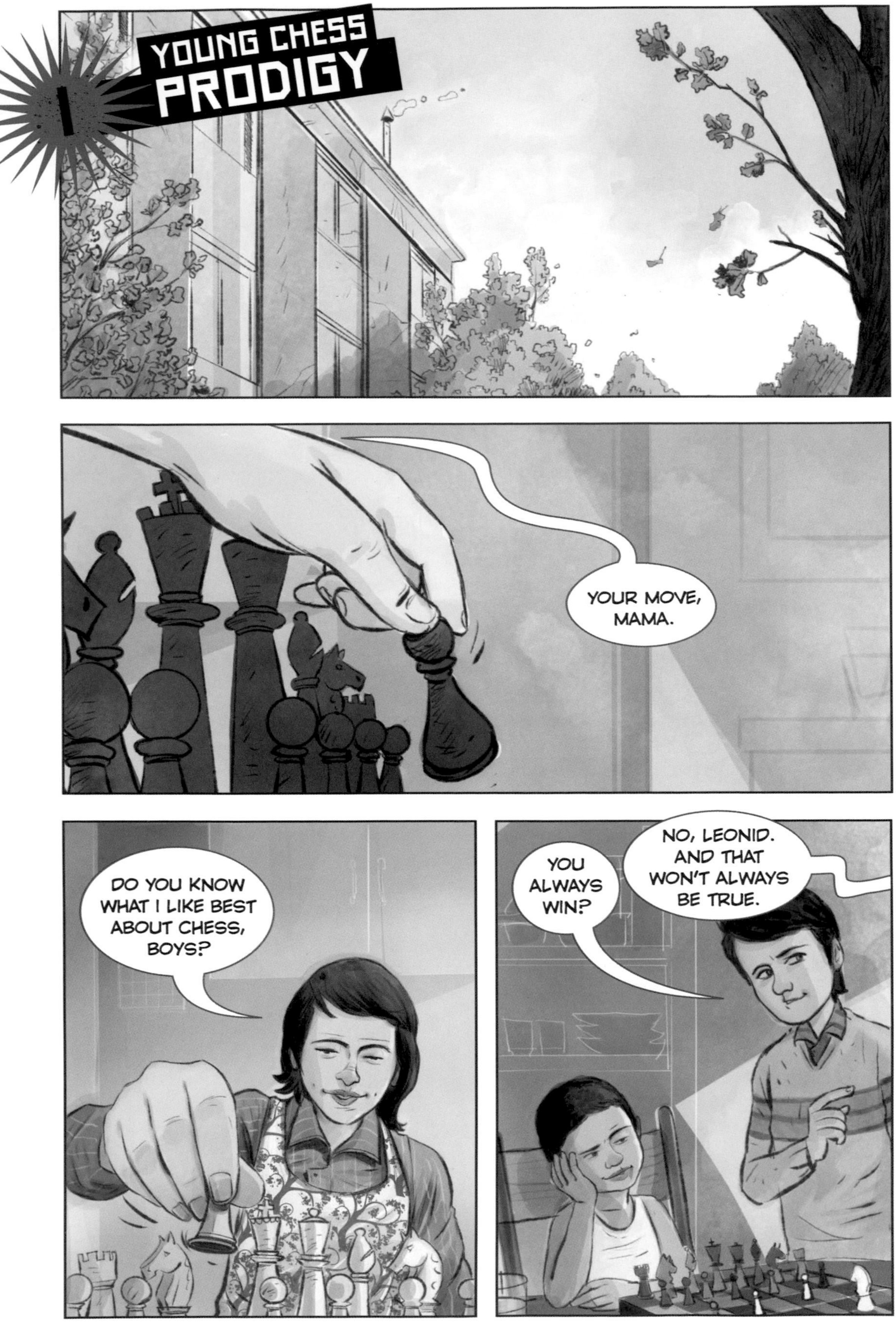
1
YOUNG CHESS PRODIGY
YOUR MOVE, MAMA.
DO YOU KNOW WHAT I LIKE BEST ABOUT CHESS, BOYS?
YOU ALWAYS WIN?
NO, LEONID. AND THAT WON'T ALWAYS BE TRUE.

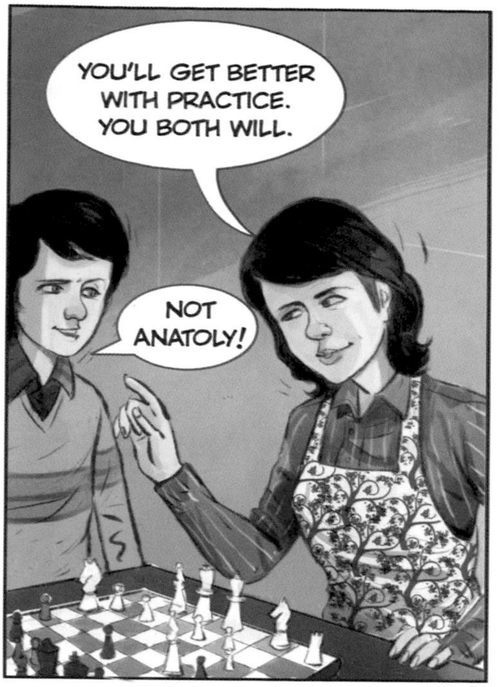
YOU'LL GET BETTER WITH PRACTICE. YOU BOTH WILL.
NOT ANATOLY!

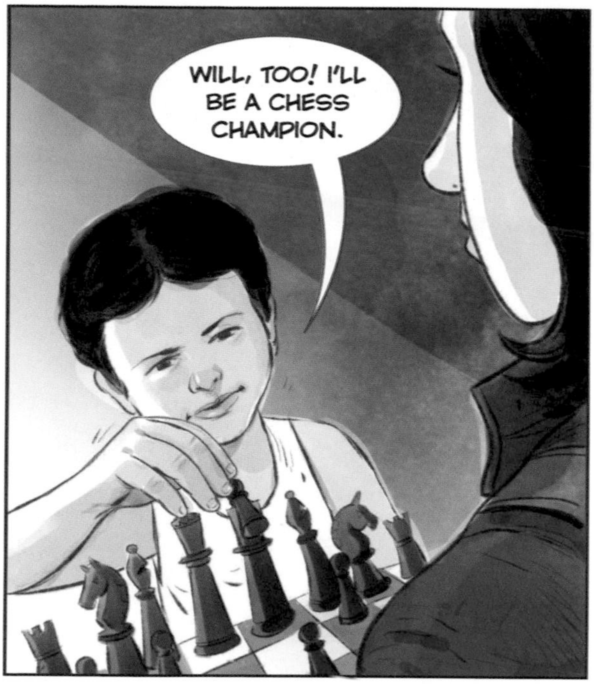
WILL, TOO! I'LL BE A CHESS CHAMPION.

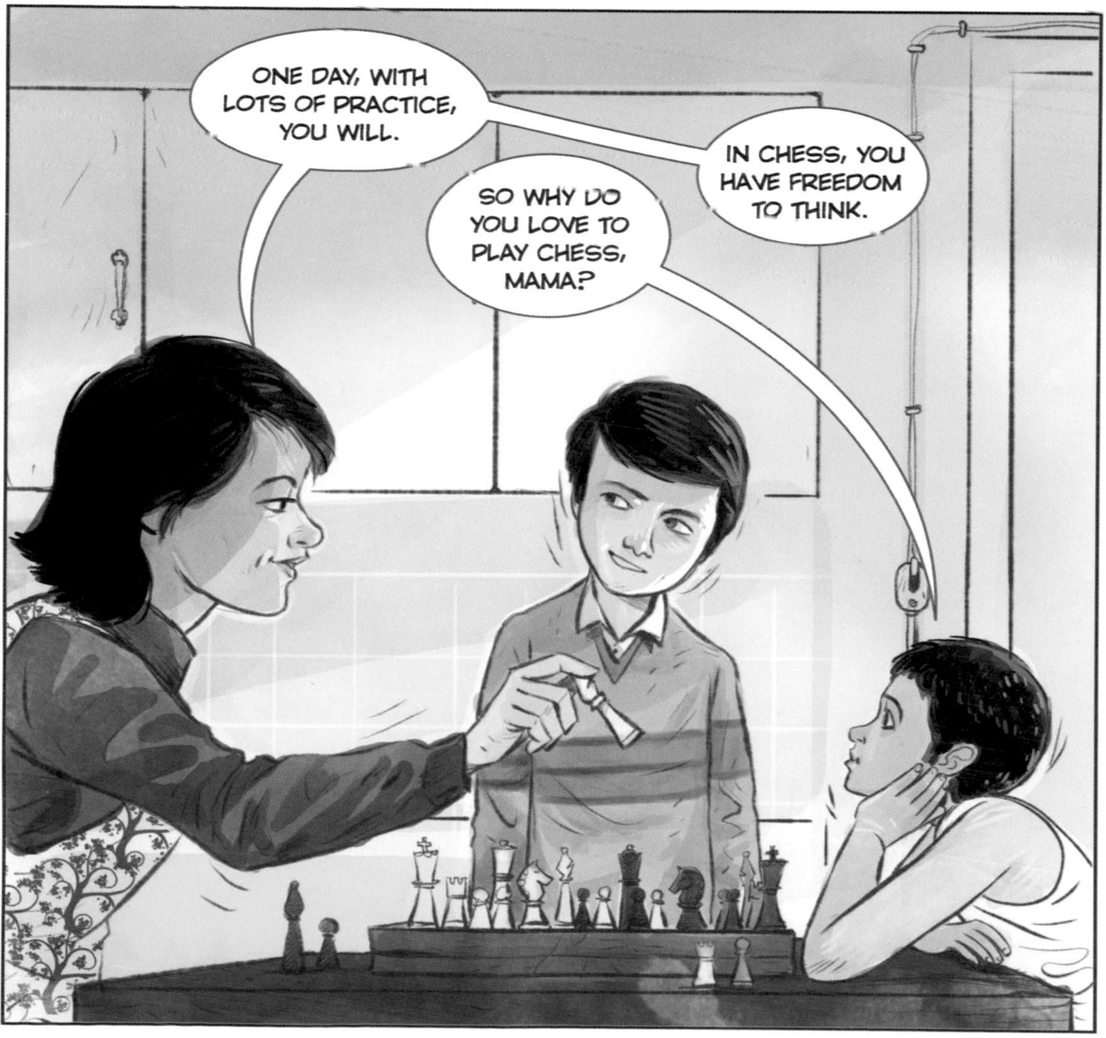
ONE DAY, WITH LOTS OF PRACTICE, YOU WILL.
SO WHY DO YOU LOVE TO PLAY CHESS, MAMA?
IN CHESS, YOU HAVE FREEDOM TO THINK.

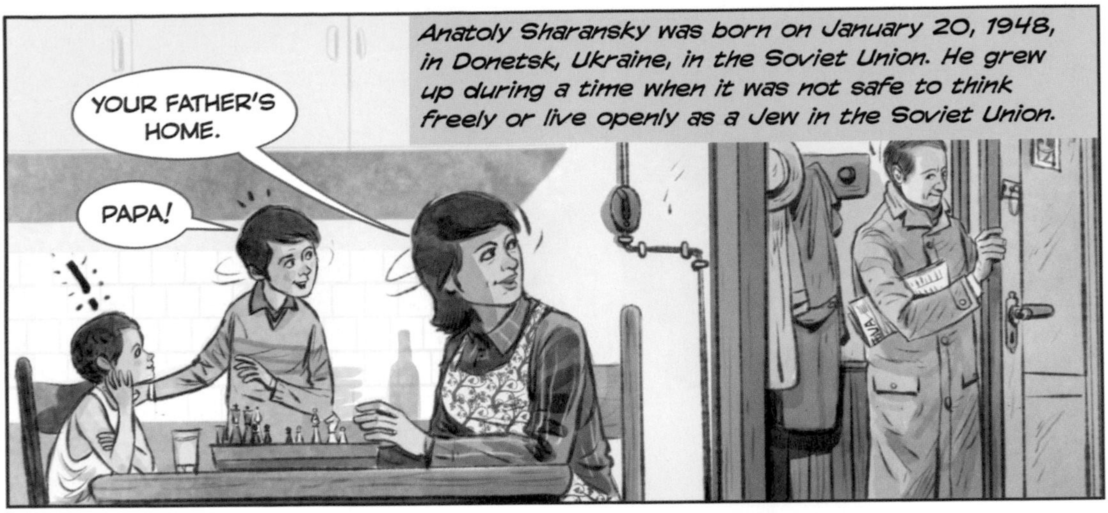
Anatoly Sharansky was born on January 20, 1948, in Donetsk, Ukraine, in the Soviet Union. He grew up during a time when it was not safe to think freely or live openly as a Jew in the Soviet Union.
YOUR FATHER'S HOME.
PAPA!

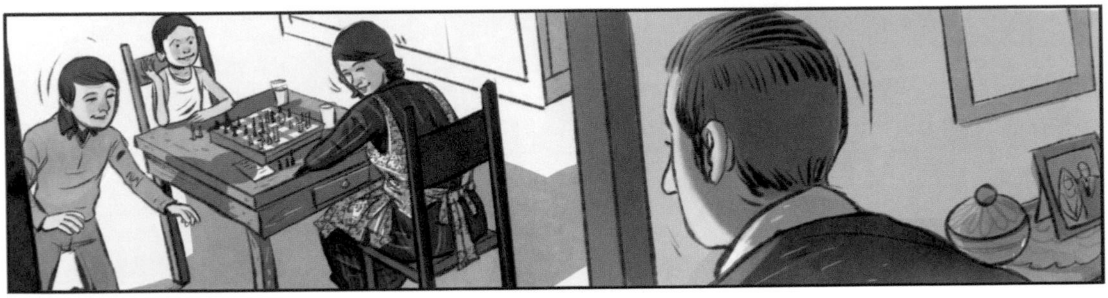

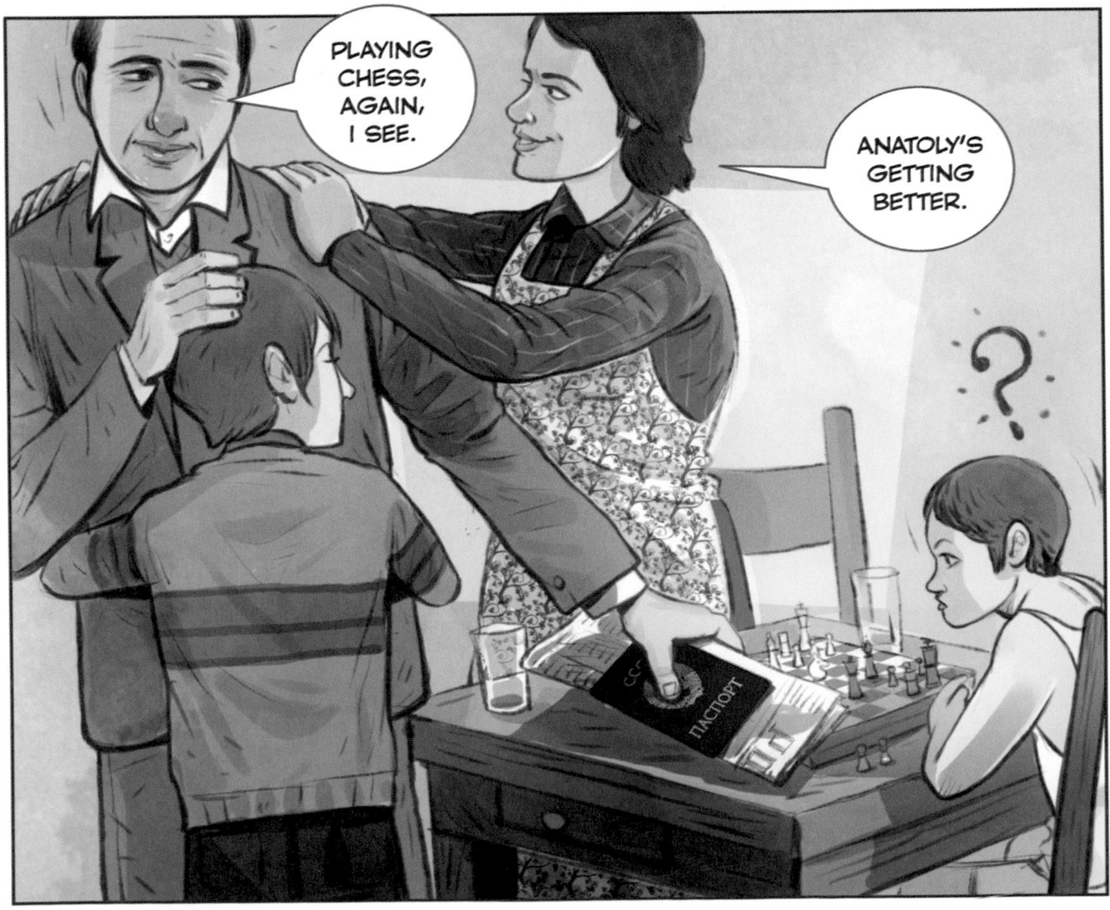
PLAYING CHESS, AGAIN, I SEE.
ANATOLY'S GETTING BETTER.
ПАСПОРТ

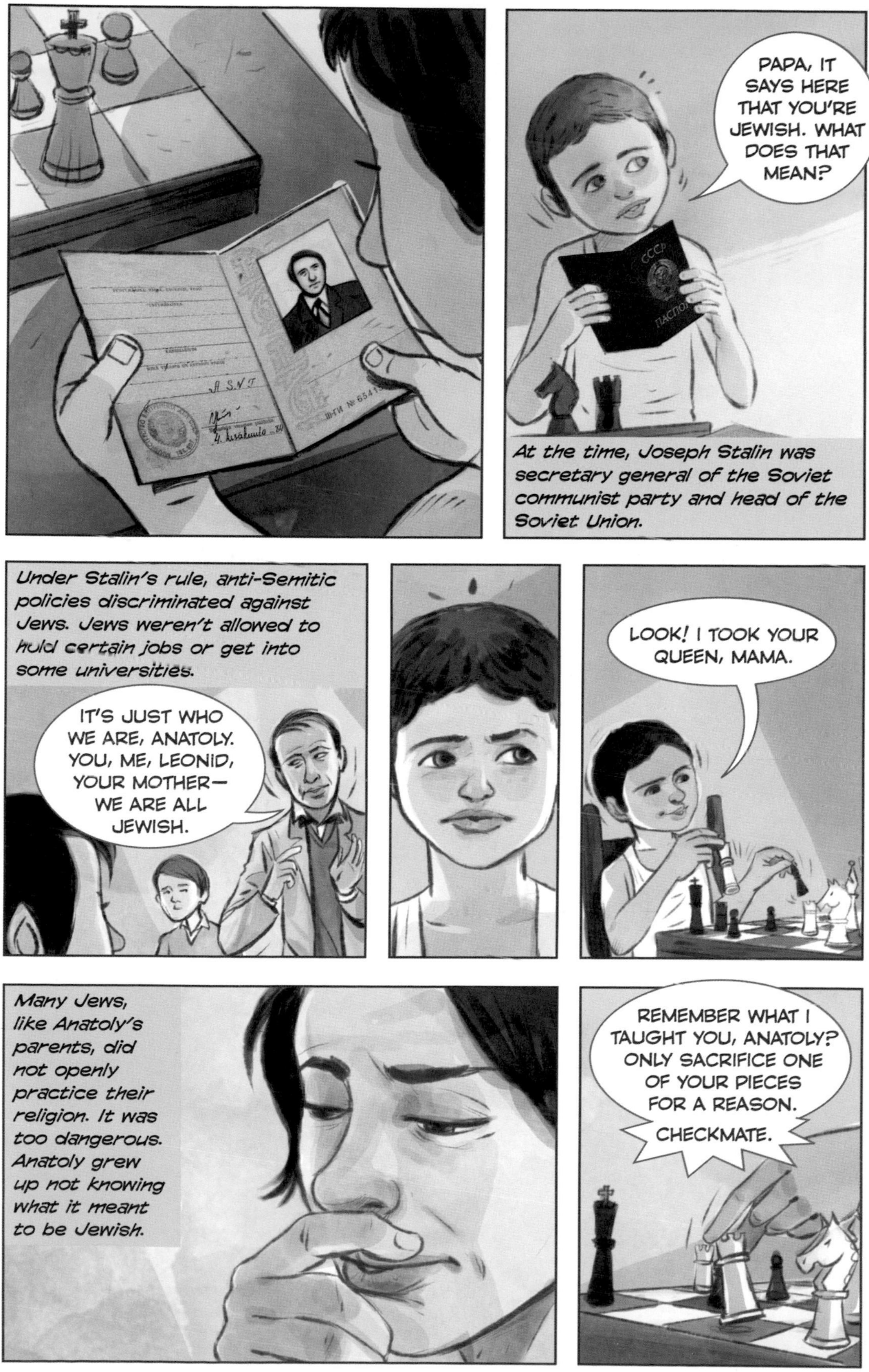
PAPA, IT SAYS HERE THAT YOU'RE JEWISH. WHAT DOES THAT MEAN?
At the time, Joseph Stalin was secretary general of the Soviet communist party and head of the Soviet Union.
Under Stalin's rule, anti-Semitic policies discriminated against Jews. Jews weren't allowed to hold certain jobs or get into some universities.
IT'S JUST WHO WE ARE, ANATOLY. YOU, ME, LEONID, YOUR MOTHER— WE ARE ALL JEWISH.
LOOK! I TOOK YOUR QUEEN, MAMA.
Many Jews, like Anatoly's parents, did not openly practice their religion. It was too dangerous. Anatoly grew up not knowing what it meant to be Jewish.
REMEMBER WHAT I TAUGHT YOU, ANATOLY? ONLY SACRIFICE ONE OF YOUR PIECES FOR A REASON.
CHECKMATE.

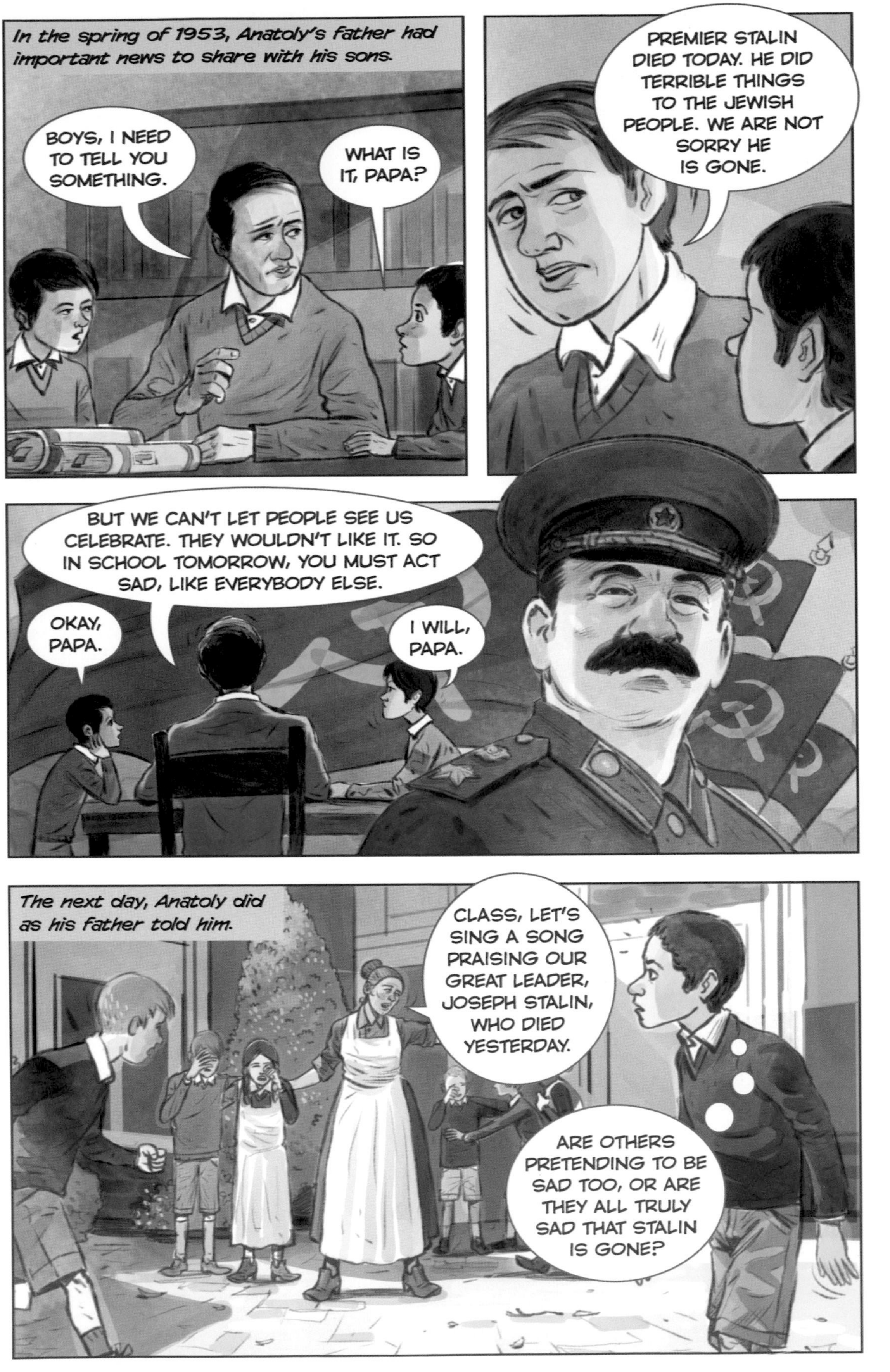
In the spring of 1953, Anatoly's father had important news to share with his sons.
BOYS, I NEED TO TELL YOU SOMETHING.
WHAT IS IT, PAPA?
PREMIER STALIN DIED TODAY. HE DID TERRIBLE THINGS TO THE JEWISH PEOPLE. WE ARE NOT SORRY HE IS GONE.
BUT WE CAN'T LET PEOPLE SEE US CELEBRATE. THEY WOULDN'T LIKE IT. SO IN SCHOOL TOMORROW, YOU MUST ACT SAD, LIKE EVERYBODY ELSE.
OKAY, PAPA.
I WILL, PAPA.
The next day, Anatoly did as his father told him.
CLASS, LET'S SING A SONG PRAISING OUR GREAT LEADER, JOSEPH STALIN, WHO DIED YESTERDAY.
ARE OTHERS PRETENDING TO BE SAD TOO, OR ARE THEY ALL TRULY SAD THAT STALIN IS GONE?

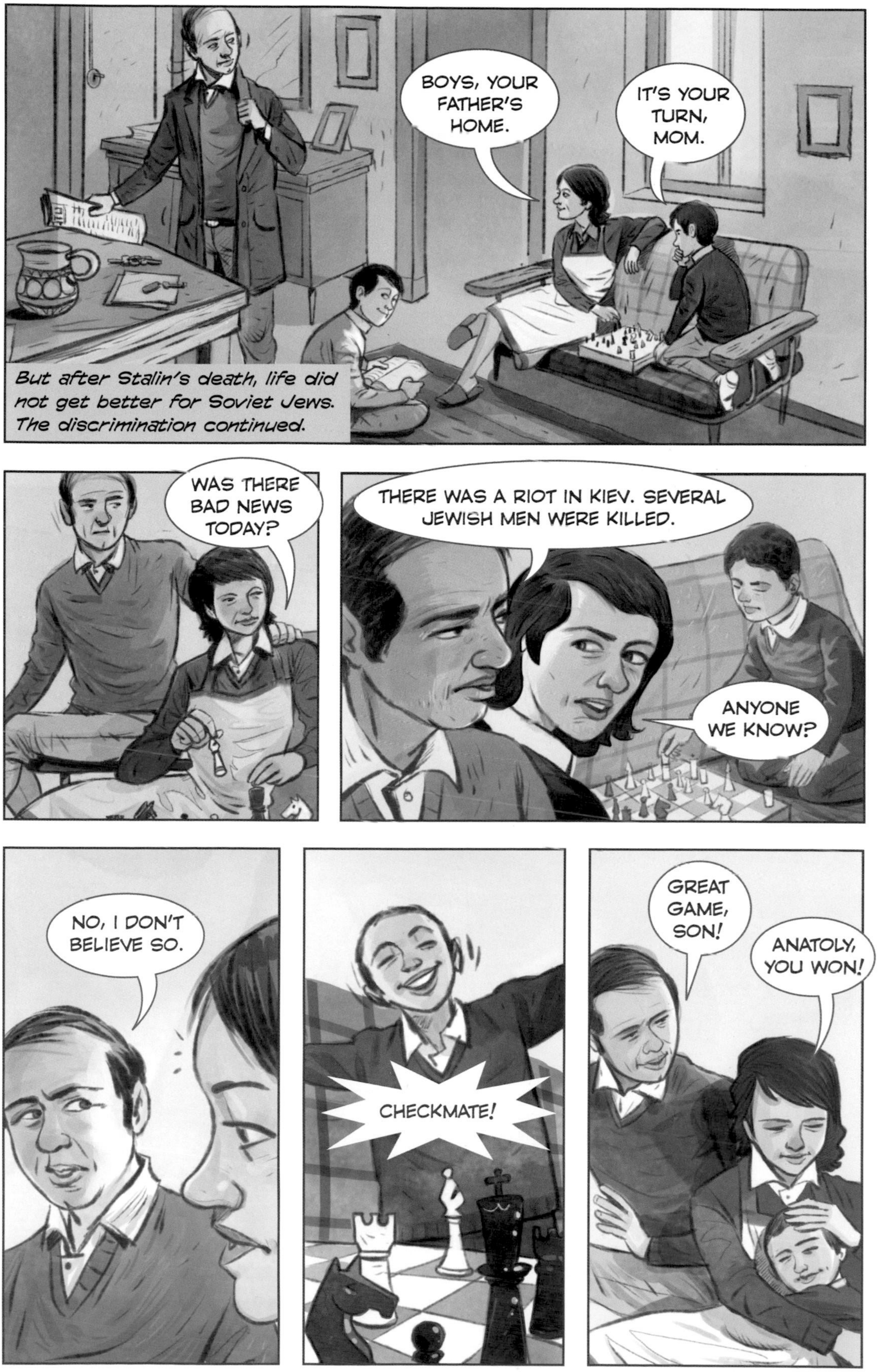
BOYS, YOUR FATHER'S HOME.
IT'S YOUR TURN, MOM.
But after Stalin's death, life did not get better for Soviet Jews. The discrimination continued.
WAS THERE BAD NEWS TODAY?
THERE WAS A RIOT IN KIEV. SEVERAL JEWISH MEN WERE KILLED.
ANYONE WE KNOW?
NO, I DON'T BELIEVE SO.
CHECKMATE!
GREAT GAME, SON!
ANATOLY, YOU WON!

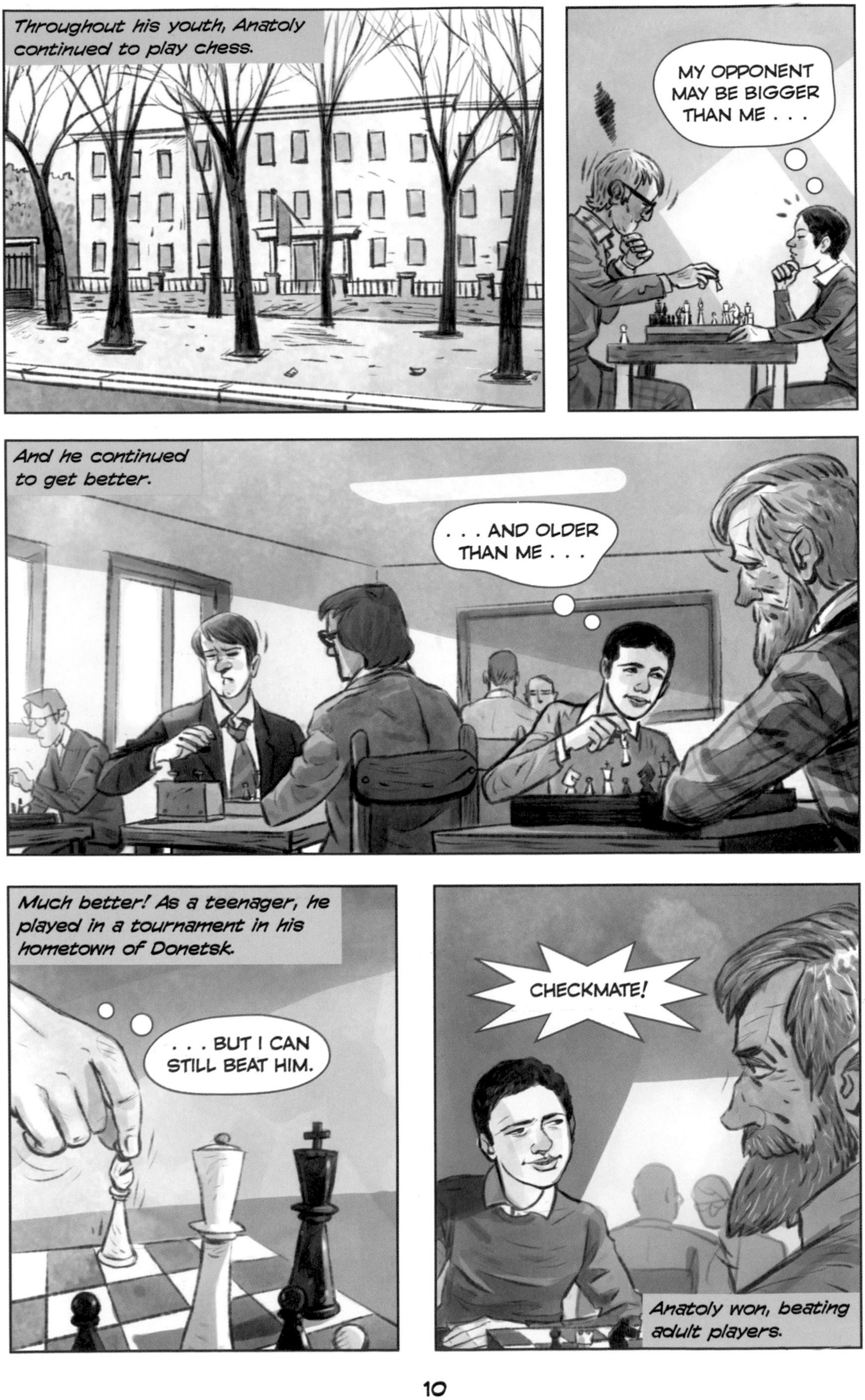
Throughout his youth, Anatoly continued to play chess.
MY OPPONENT MAY BE BIGGER THAN ME . . .
And he continued to get better.
. . . AND OLDER THAN ME . . .
Much better! As a teenager, he played in a tournament in his hometown of Donetsk.
. . . BUT I CAN STILL BEAT HIM.
CHECKMATE!
Anatoly won, beating adult players.

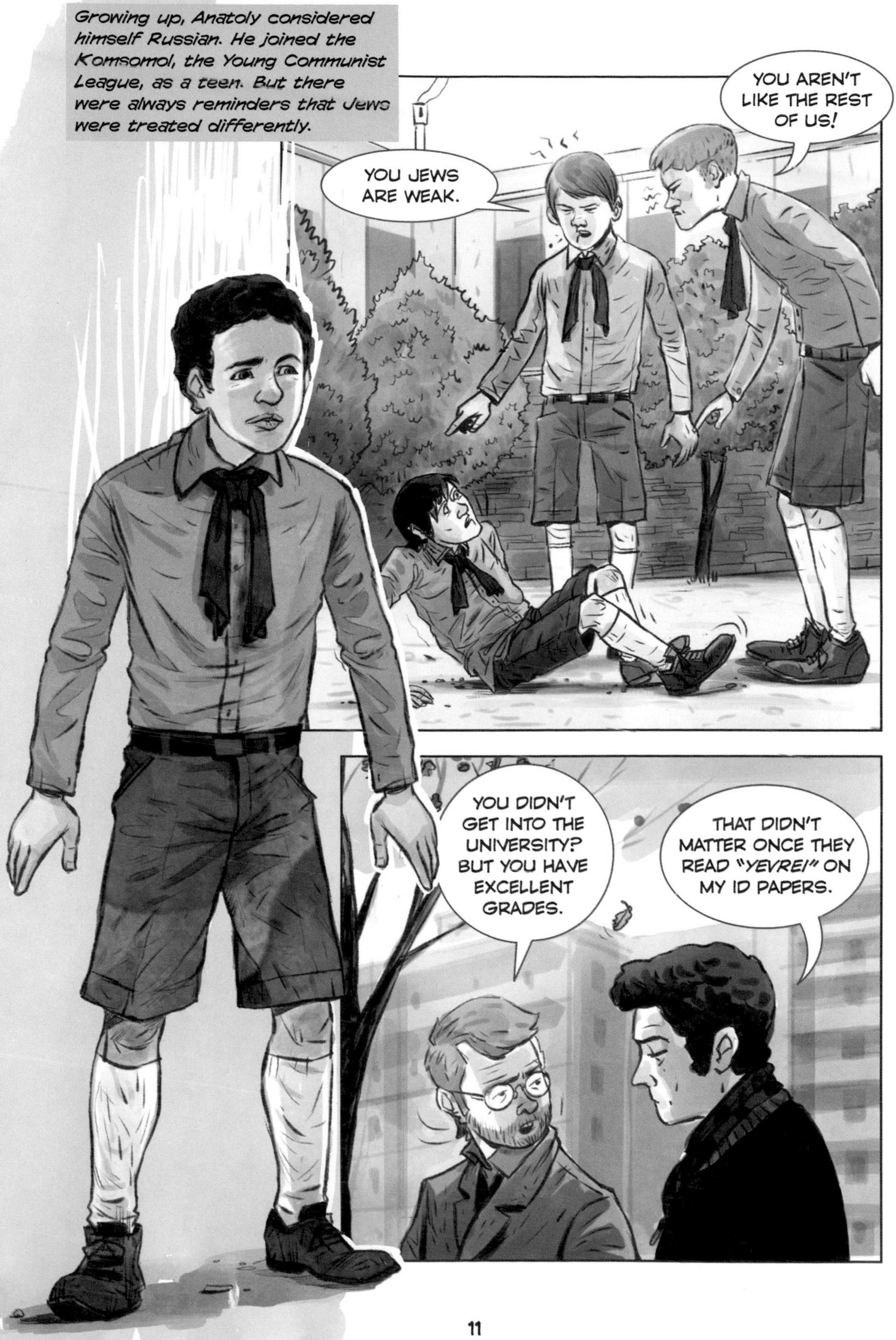

Growing up, Anatoly considered himself Russian. He joined the Komsomol, the Young Communist League, as a teen. But there were always reminders that Jews were treated differently.
YOU JEWS ARE WEAK.
YOU AREN'T LIKE THE REST OF US!
YOU DIDN'T GET INTO THE UNIVERSITY? BUT YOU HAVE EXCELLENT GRADES.
THAT DIDN'T MATTER ONCE THEY READ "YEVREI" ON MY ID PAPERS.

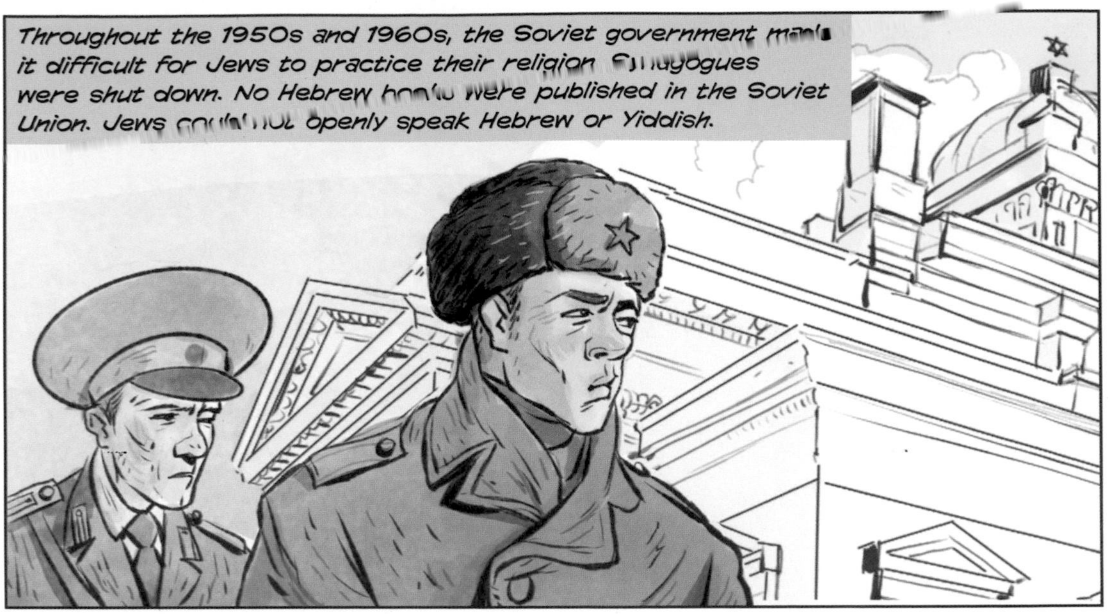
Throughout the 1950s and 1960s, the Soviet government made it difficult for Jews to practice their religion. Synagogues were shut down. No Hebrew books were published in the Soviet Union. Jews could not openly speak Hebrew or Yiddish.

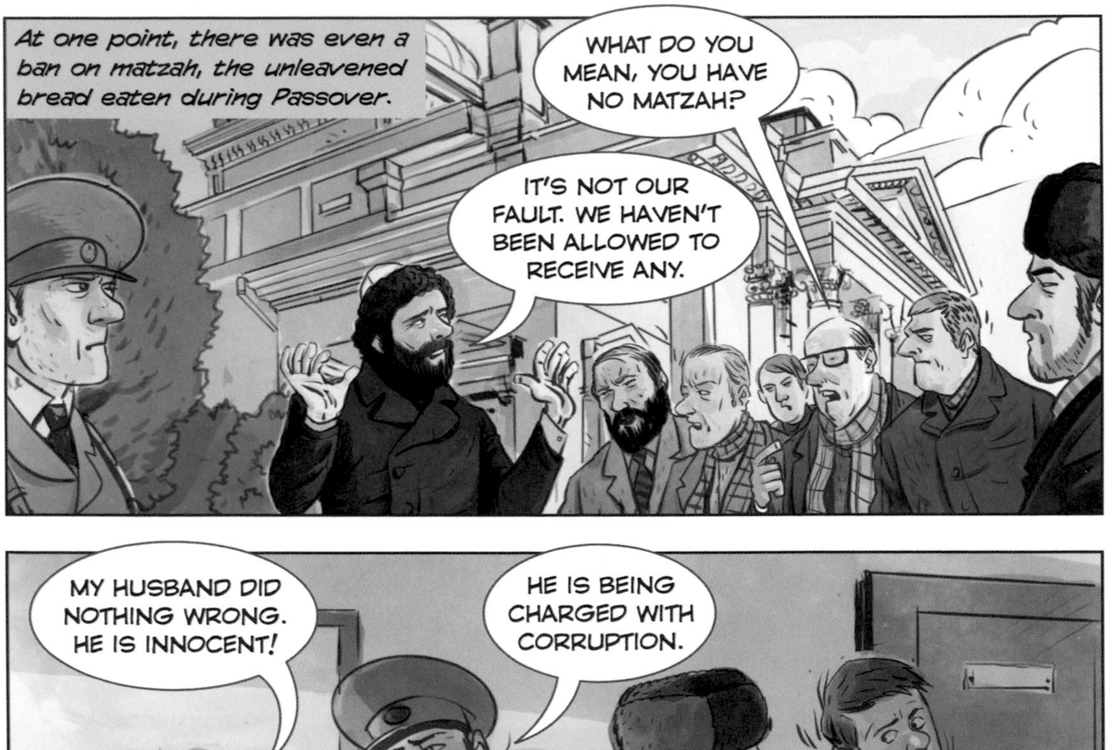
At one point, there was even a ban on matzah, the unleavened bread eaten during Passover.
WHAT DO YOU MEAN, YOU HAVE NO MATZAH?
IT'S NOT OUR FAULT. WE HAVEN'T BEEN ALLOWED TO RECEIVE ANY.

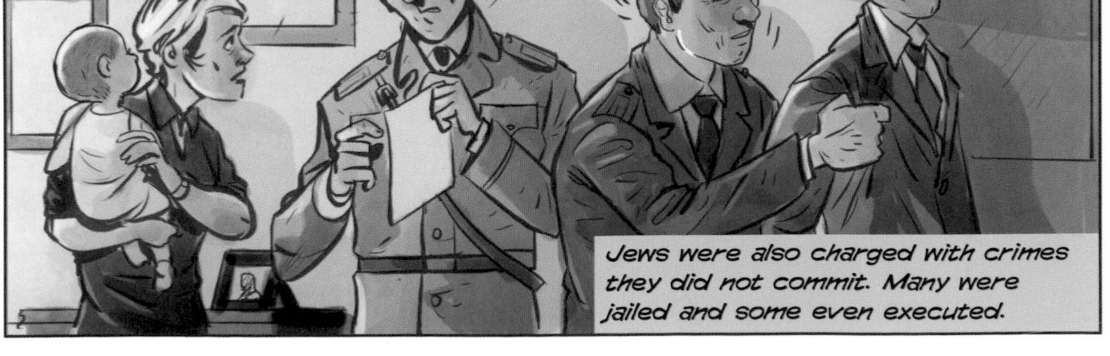
MY HUSBAND DID NOTHING WRONG. HE IS INNOCENT!
HE IS BEING CHARGED WITH CORRUPTION.
Jews were also charged with crimes they did not commit. Many were jailed and some even executed.

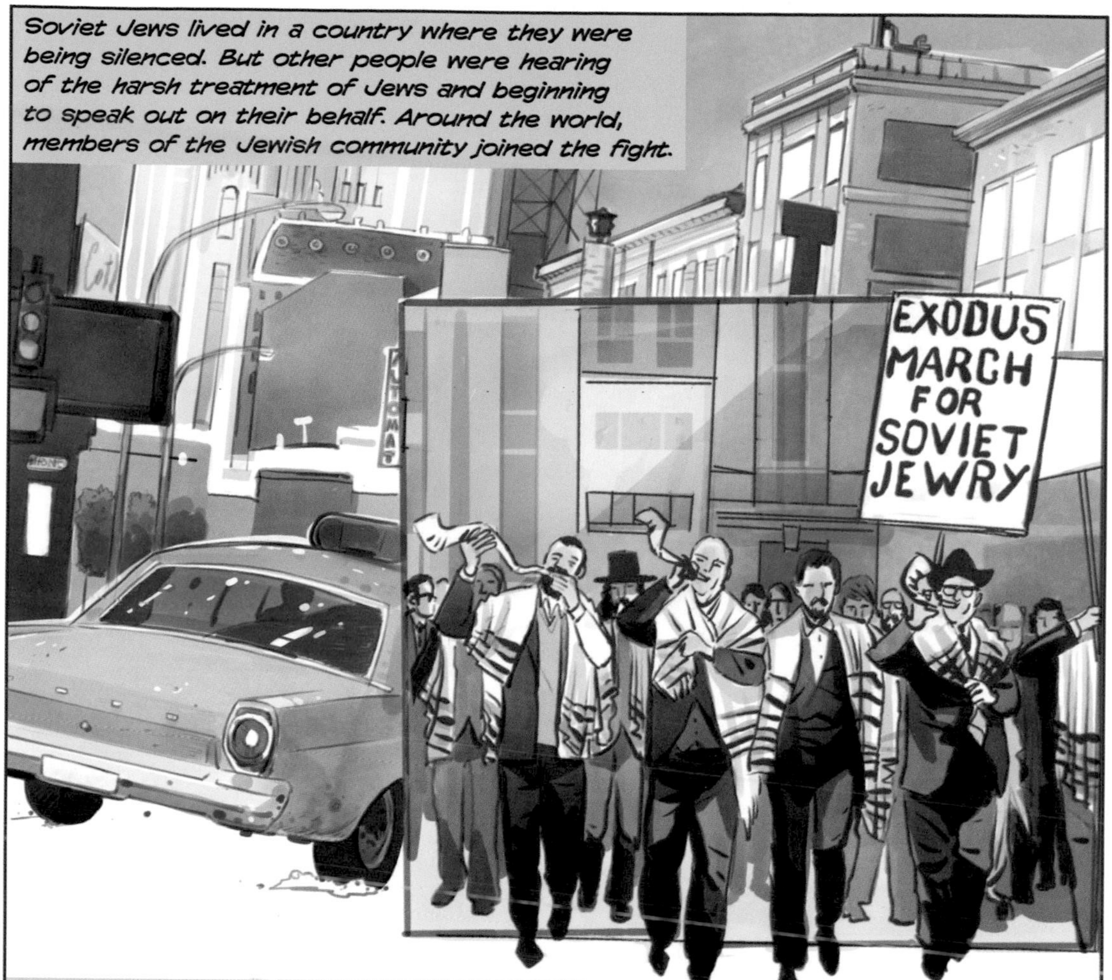
Soviet Jews lived in a country where they were being silenced. But other people were hearing of the harsh treatment of Jews and beginning to speak out on their behalf. Around the world, members of the Jewish community joined the fight.
EXODUS MARCH FOR SOVIET JEWRY

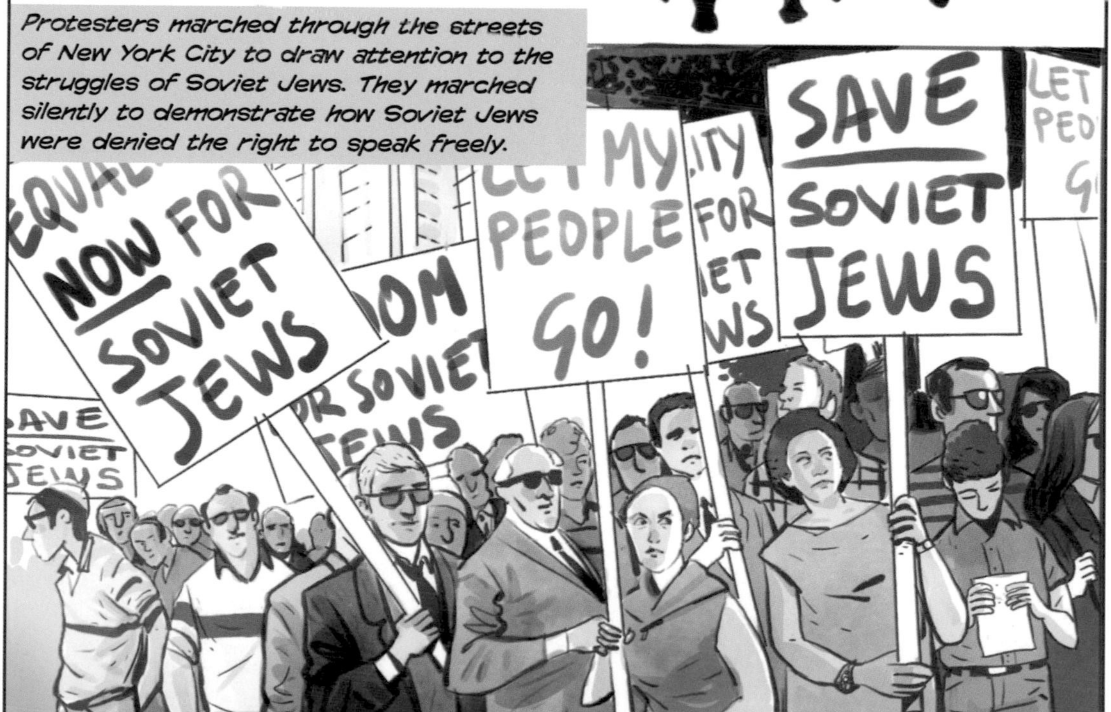
Protesters marched through the streets of New York City to draw attention to the struggles of Soviet Jews. They marched silently to demonstrate how Soviet Jews were denied the right to speak freely.
NOW FOR SOVIET JEWS
PEOPLE GO!
SAVE SOVIET JEWS
SAVE SOVIET JEWS

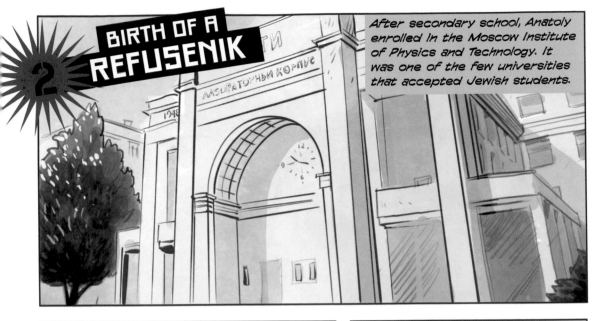

BIRTH OF A REFUSENIK

After secondary school, Anatoly enrolled in the Moscow Institute of Physics and Technology. It was one of the few universities that accepted Jewish students.

Anatoly was an exceptional student.

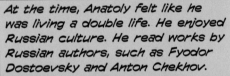

At the time, Anatoly felt like he was living a double life. He enjoyed Russian culture. He read works by Russian authors, such as Fyodor Dostoevsky and Anton Chekhov.

Yet, he found it harder and harder to deny his Jewish heritage.

I HEARD RUMORS THAT EGYPT IS PLANNING TO CLOSE THE STRAITS OF TIRAN TO STOP ISRAELI SHIPS FROM REACHING THE RED SEA.

TRUST ME. THERE WILL BE WAR IF THAT HAPPENS.

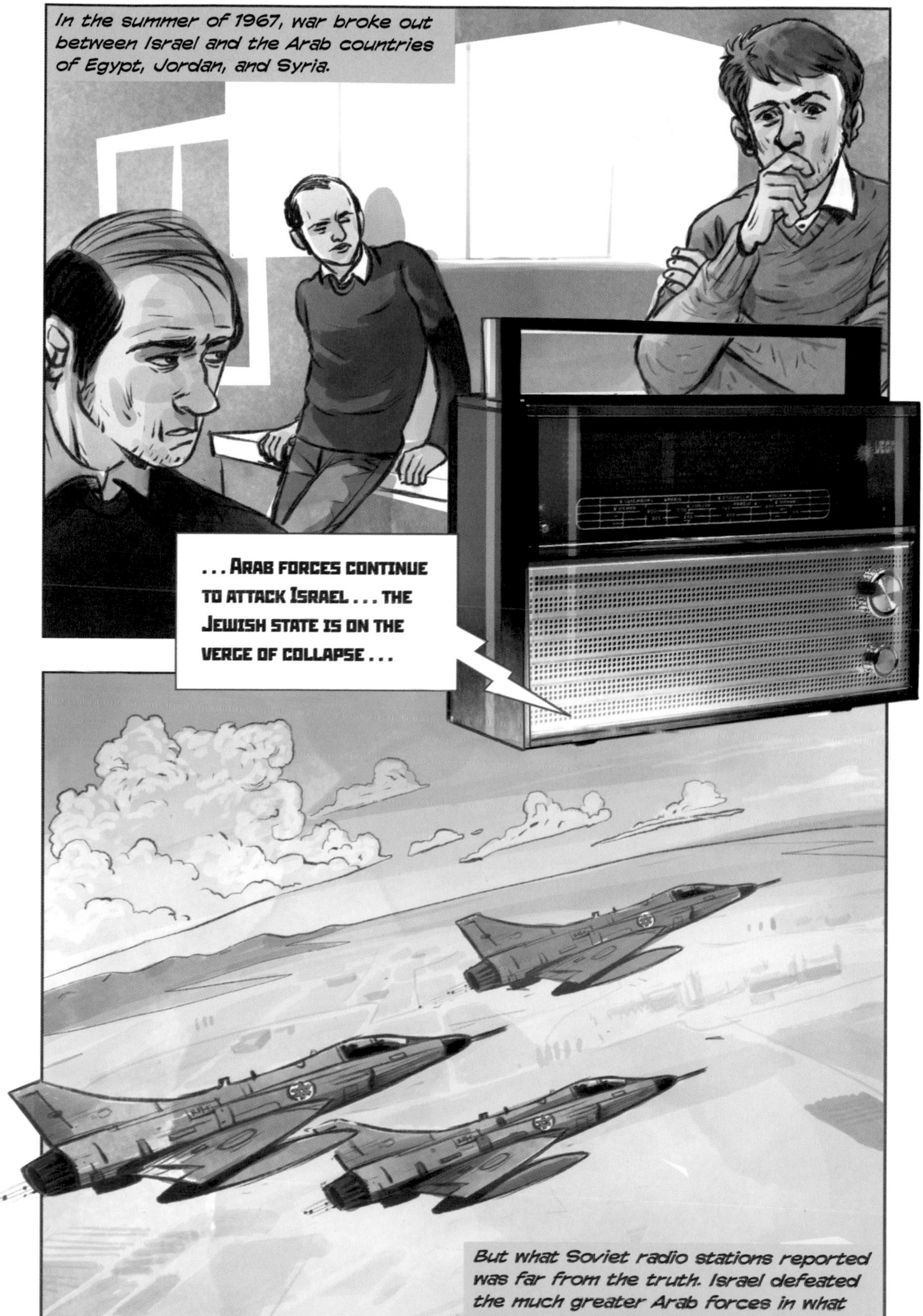
In the summer of 1967, war broke out between Israel and the Arab countries of Egypt, Jordan, and Syria.
. . . Arab forces continue to attack Israel . . . the Jewish state is on the verge of collapse . . .
But what Soviet radio stations reported was far from the truth. Israel defeated the much greater Arab forces in what became known as the Six-Day War.

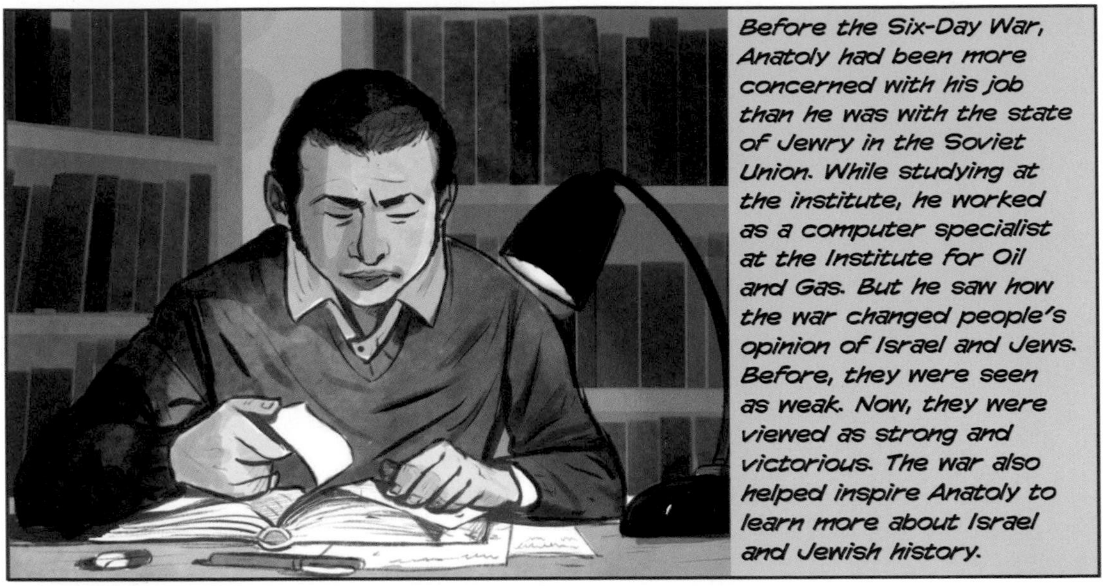
Before the Six-Day War, Anatoly had been more concerned with his job than he was with the state of Jewry in the Soviet Union. While studying at the institute, he worked as a computer specialist at the Institute for Oil and Gas. But he saw how the war changed people's opinion of Israel and Jews. Before, they were seen as weak. Now, they were viewed as strong and victorious. The war also helped inspire Anatoly to learn more about Israel and Jewish history.

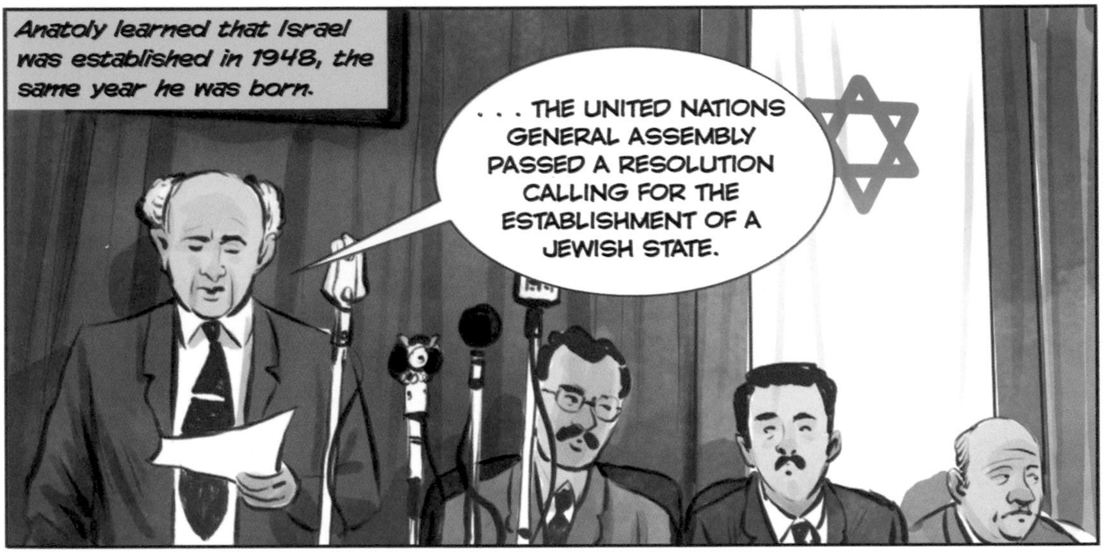
Anatoly learned that Israel was established in 1948, the same year he was born.
. . . THE UNITED NATIONS GENERAL ASSEMBLY PASSED A RESOLUTION CALLING FOR THE ESTABLISHMENT OF A JEWISH STATE.

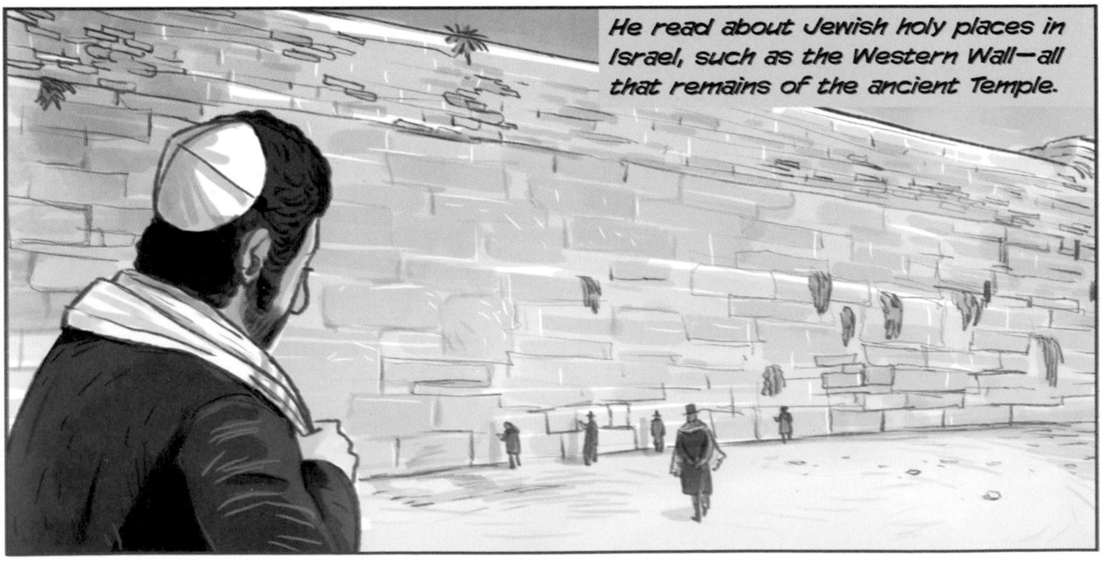
He read about Jewish holy places in Israel, such as the Western Wall—all that remains of the ancient Temple.

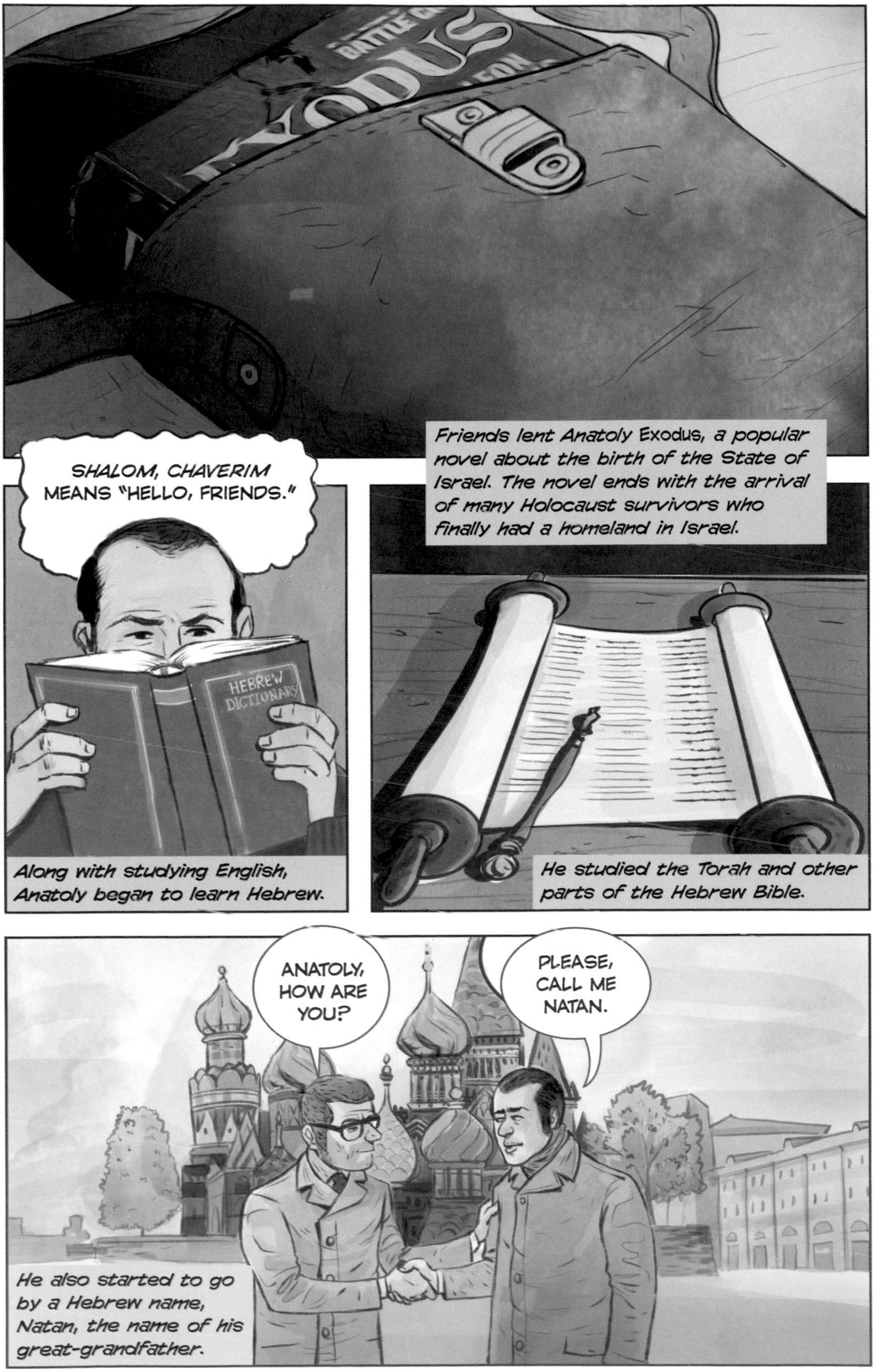
BATTLE CRY
EXODUS
Friends lent Anatoly Exodus, a popular novel about the birth of the State of Israel. The novel ends with the arrival of many Holocaust survivors who finally had a homeland in Israel.
SHALOM, CHAVERIM MEANS "HELLO, FRIENDS."
HEBREW DICTIONARY
Along with studying English, Anatoly began to learn Hebrew.
He studied the Torah and other parts of the Hebrew Bible.
ANATOLY, HOW ARE YOU?
PLEASE, CALL ME NATAN.
He also started to go by a Hebrew name, Natan, the name of his great-grandfather.

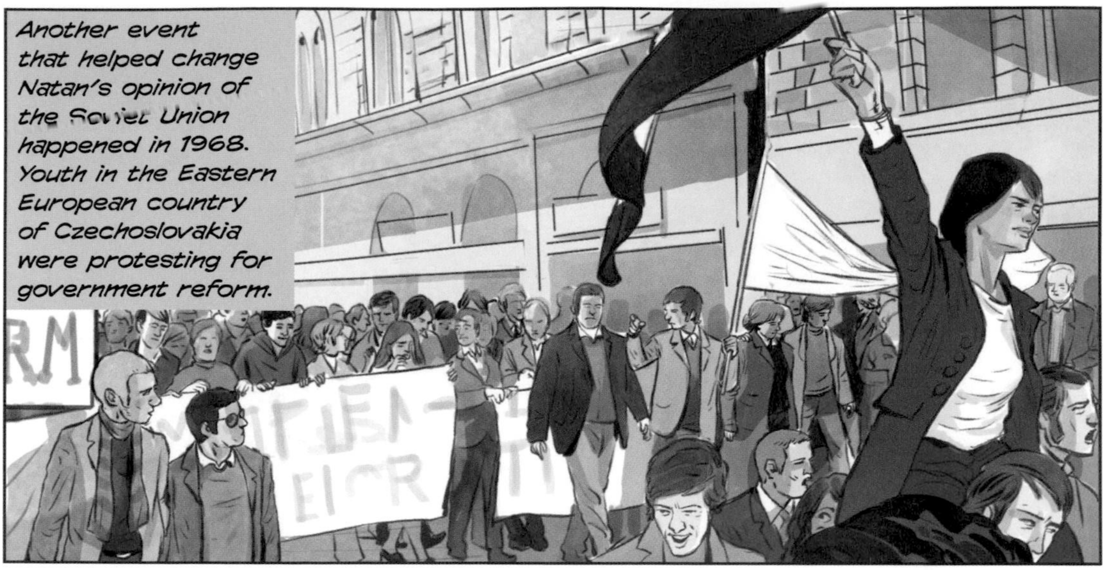
Another event that helped change Natan's opinion of the Soviet Union happened in 1968. Youth in the Eastern European country of Czechoslovakia were protesting for government reform.

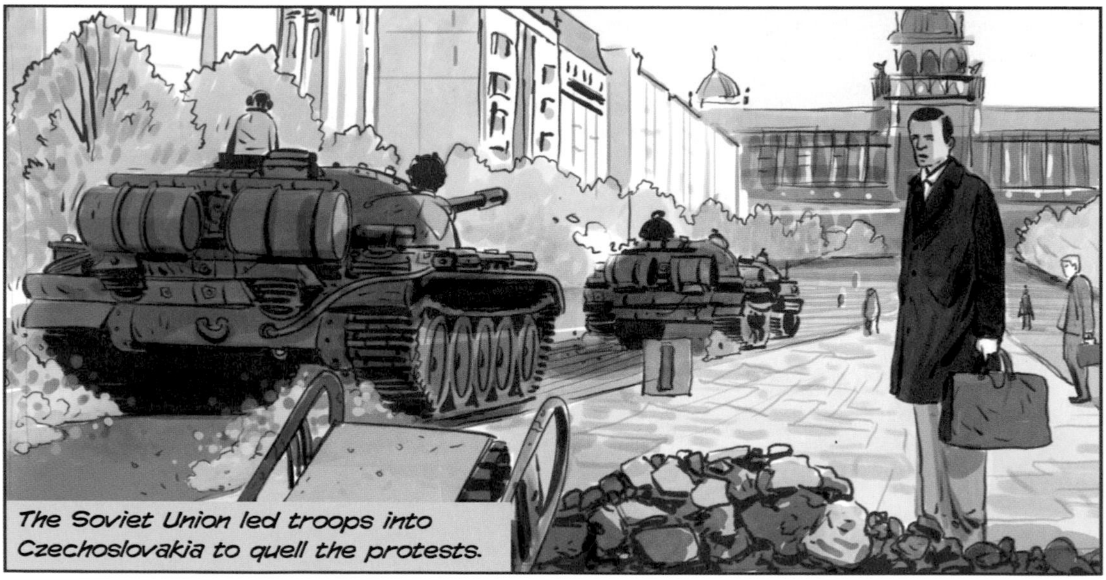
The Soviet Union led troops into Czechoslovakia to quell the protests.

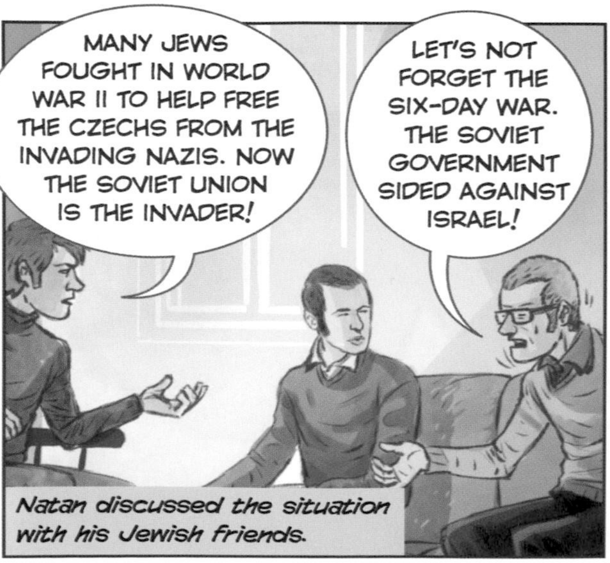
MANY JEWS FOUGHT IN WORLD WAR II TO HELP FREE THE CZECHS FROM THE INVADING NAZIS. NOW THE SOVIET UNION IS THE INVADER!
LET'S NOT FORGET THE SIX-DAY WAR. THE SOVIET GOVERNMENT SIDED AGAINST ISRAEL!
Natan discussed the situation with his Jewish friends.

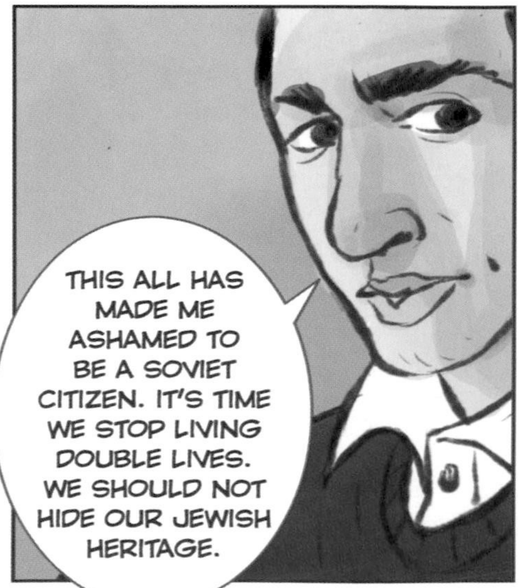
THIS ALL HAS MADE ME ASHAMED TO BE A SOVIET CITIZEN. IT'S TIME WE STOP LIVING DOUBLE LIVES. WE SHOULD NOT HIDE OUR JEWISH HERITAGE.

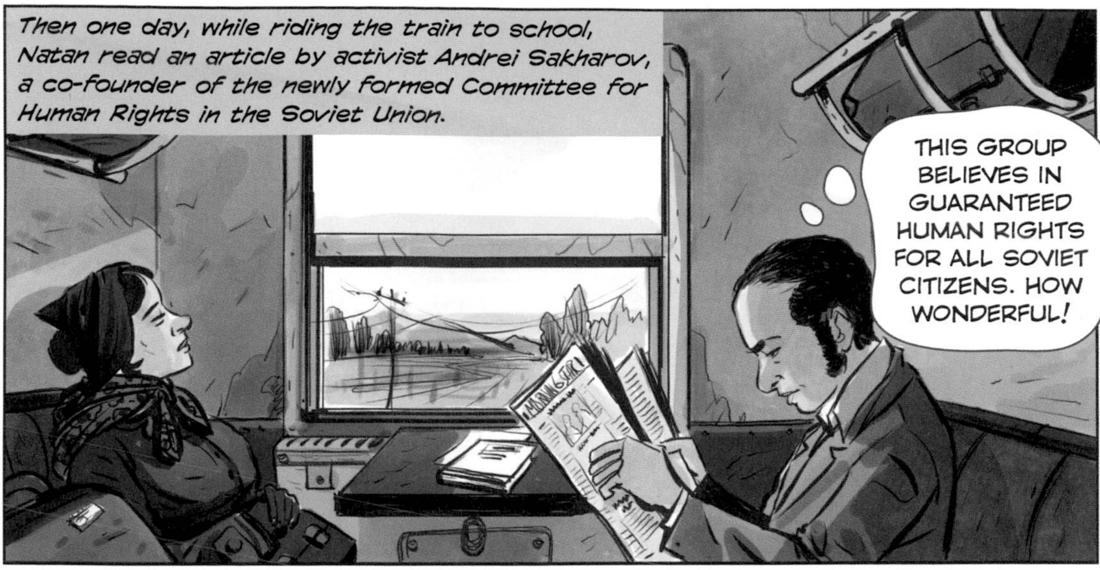
Then one day, while riding the train to school, Natan read an article by activist Andrei Sakharov, a co-founder of the newly formed Committee for Human Rights in the Soviet Union.
THIS GROUP BELIEVES IN GUARANTEED HUMAN RIGHTS FOR ALL SOVIET CITIZENS. HOW WONDERFUL!

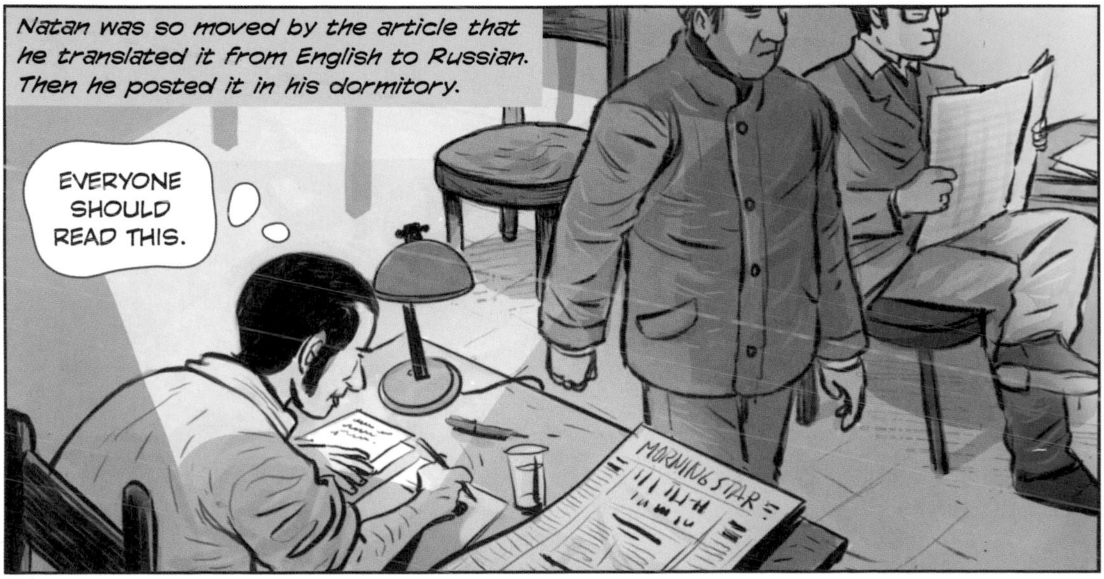
Natan was so moved by the article that he translated it from English to Russian. Then he posted it in his dormitory.
EVERYONE SHOULD READ THIS.
MORNING STAR

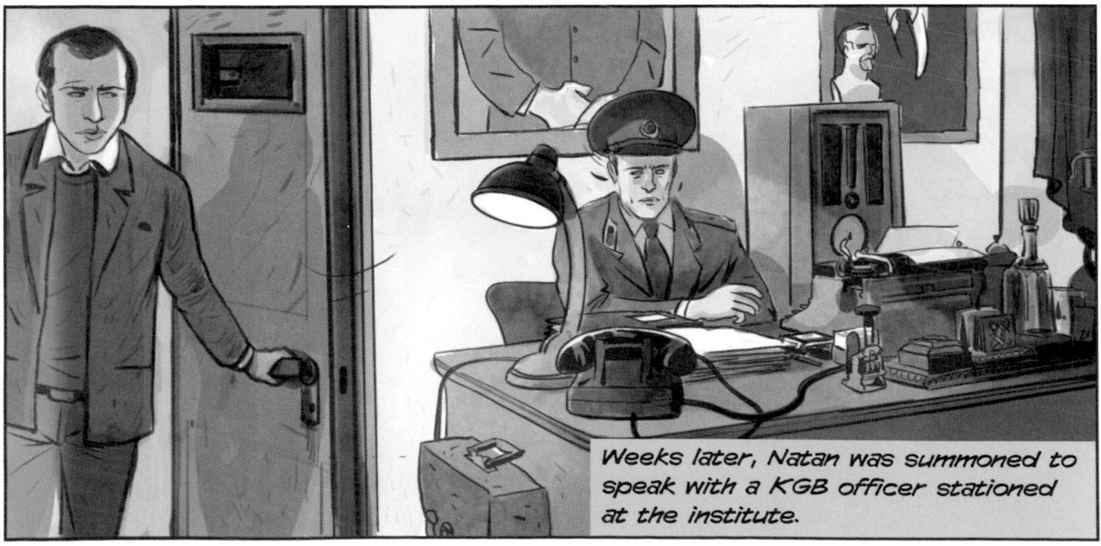
Weeks later, Natan was summoned to speak with a KGB officer stationed at the institute.

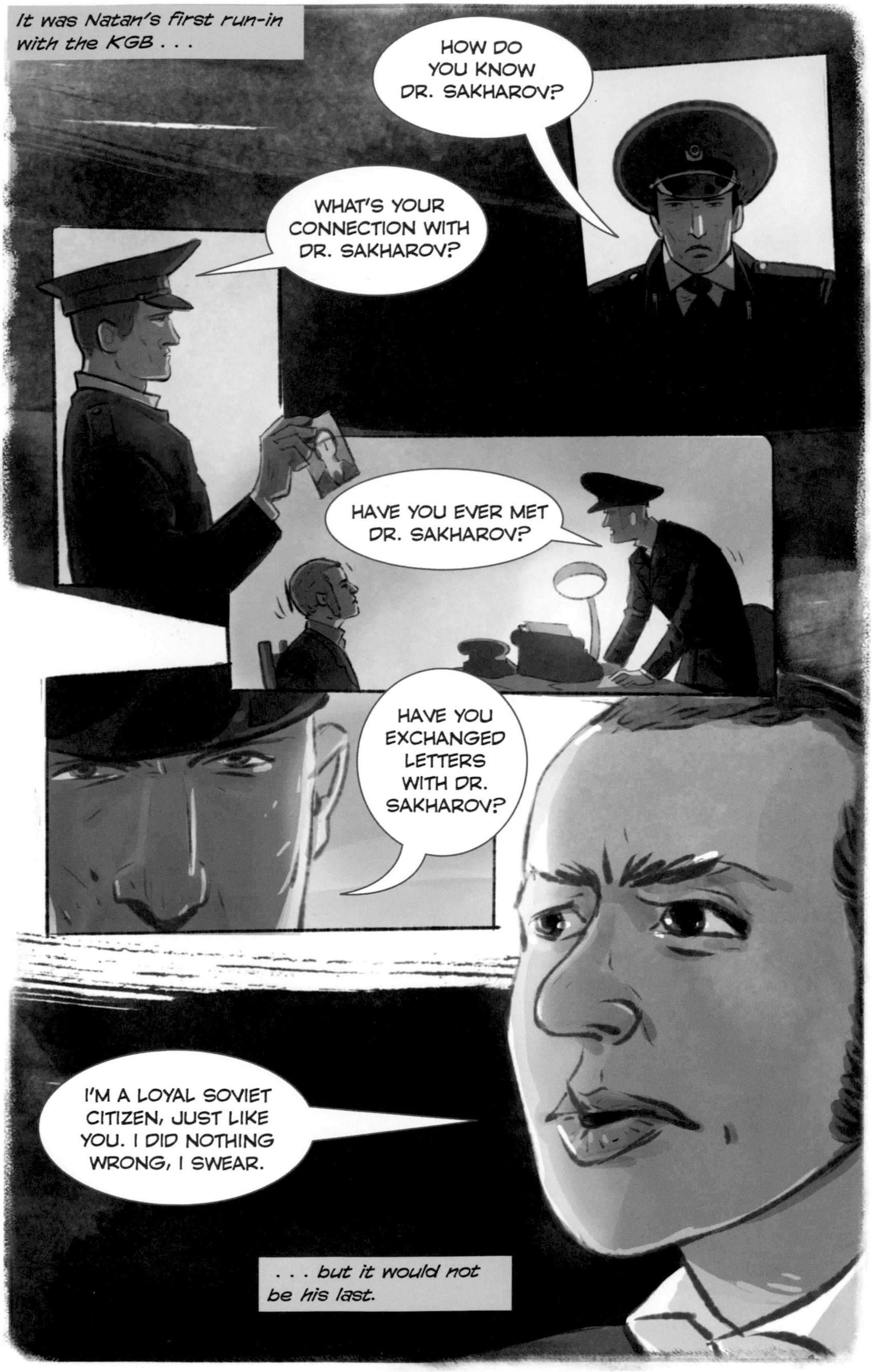
It was Natan's first run-in with the KGB . . .
HOW DO YOU KNOW DR. SAKHAROV?
WHAT'S YOUR CONNECTION WITH DR. SAKHAROV?
HAVE YOU EVER MET DR. SAKHAROV?
HAVE YOU EXCHANGED LETTERS WITH DR. SAKHAROV?
I'M A LOYAL SOVIET CITIZEN, JUST LIKE YOU. I DID NOTHING WRONG, I SWEAR.
. . . but it would not be his last.

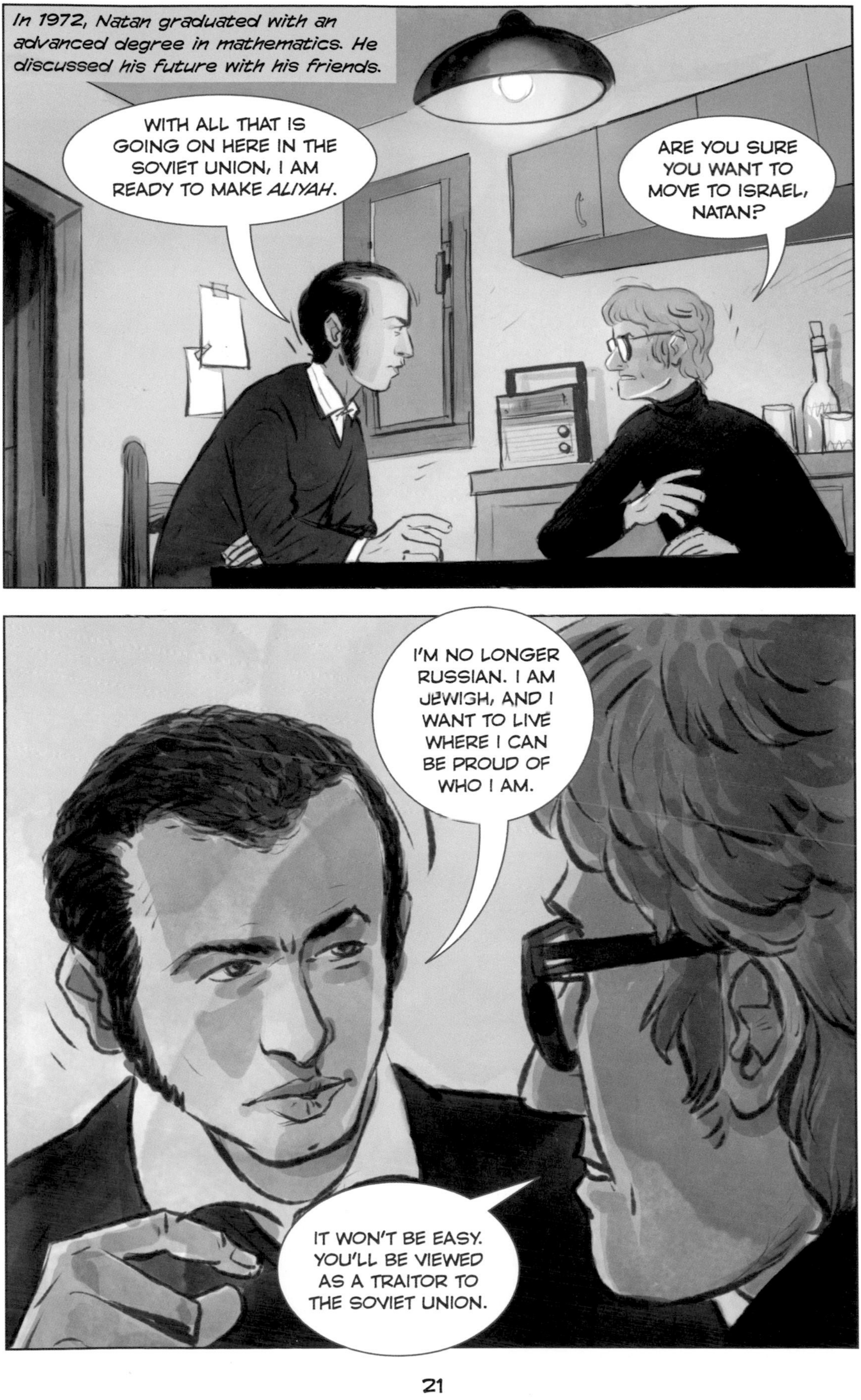
In 1972, Natan graduated with an advanced degree in mathematics. He discussed his future with his friends.
WITH ALL THAT IS GOING ON HERE IN THE SOVIET UNION, I AM READY TO MAKE *ALIYAH*.
ARE YOU SURE YOU WANT TO MOVE TO ISRAEL, NATAN?
I'M NO LONGER RUSSIAN. I AM JEWISH, AND I WANT TO LIVE WHERE I CAN BE PROUD OF WHO I AM.
IT WON'T BE EASY. YOU'LL BE VIEWED AS A TRAITOR TO THE SOVIET UNION.

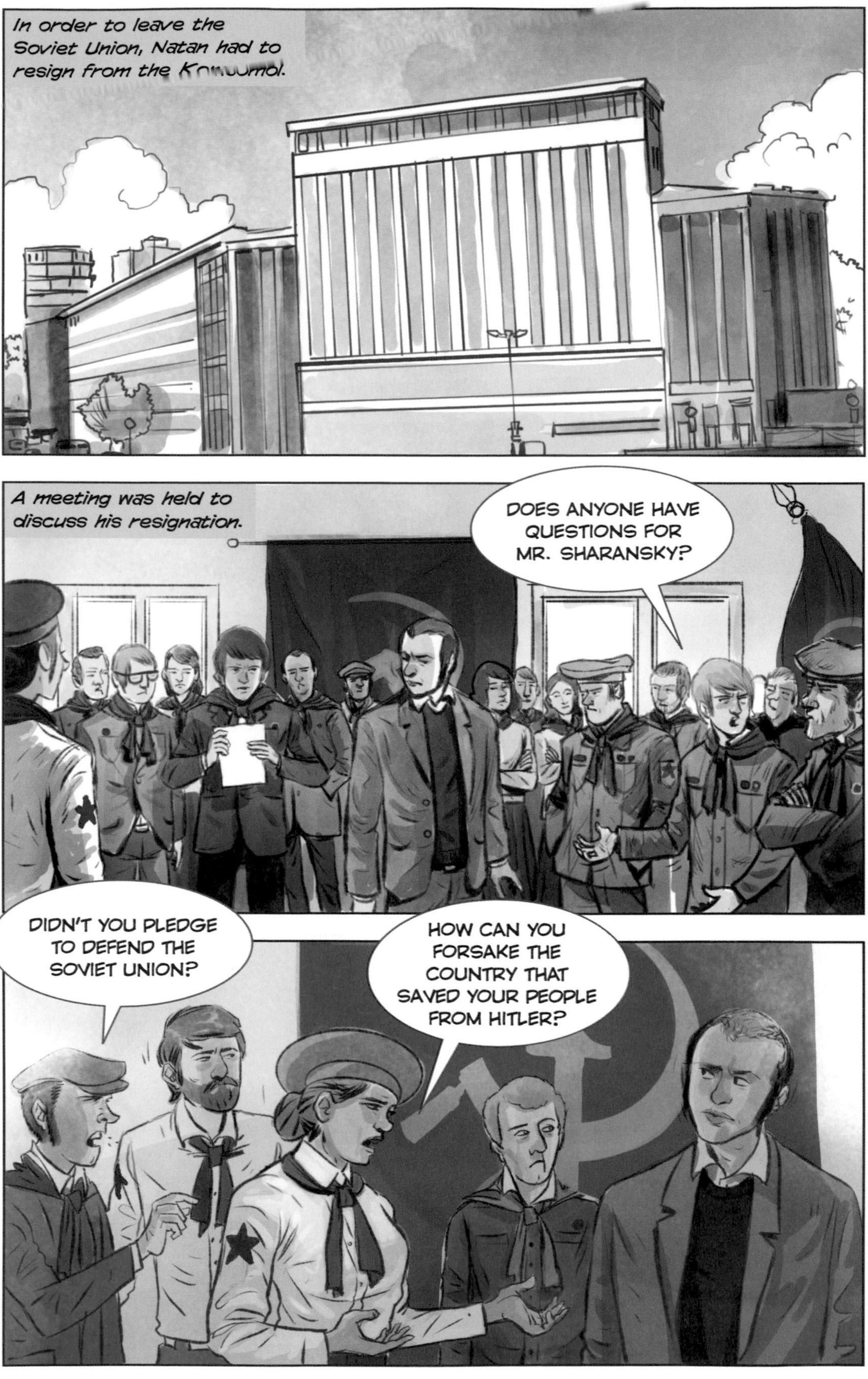
In order to leave the Soviet Union, Natan had to resign from the Komsomol.
A meeting was held to discuss his resignation.
DOES ANYONE HAVE QUESTIONS FOR MR. SHARANSKY?
DIDN'T YOU PLEDGE TO DEFEND THE SOVIET UNION?
HOW CAN YOU FORSAKE THE COUNTRY THAT SAVED YOUR PEOPLE FROM HITLER?

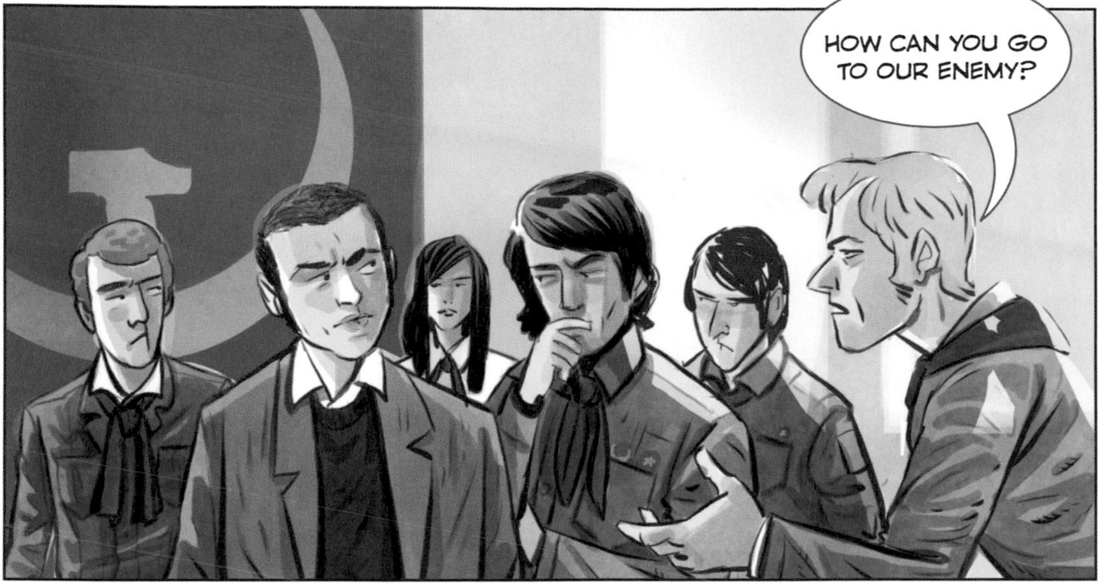
HOW CAN YOU GO TO OUR ENEMY?

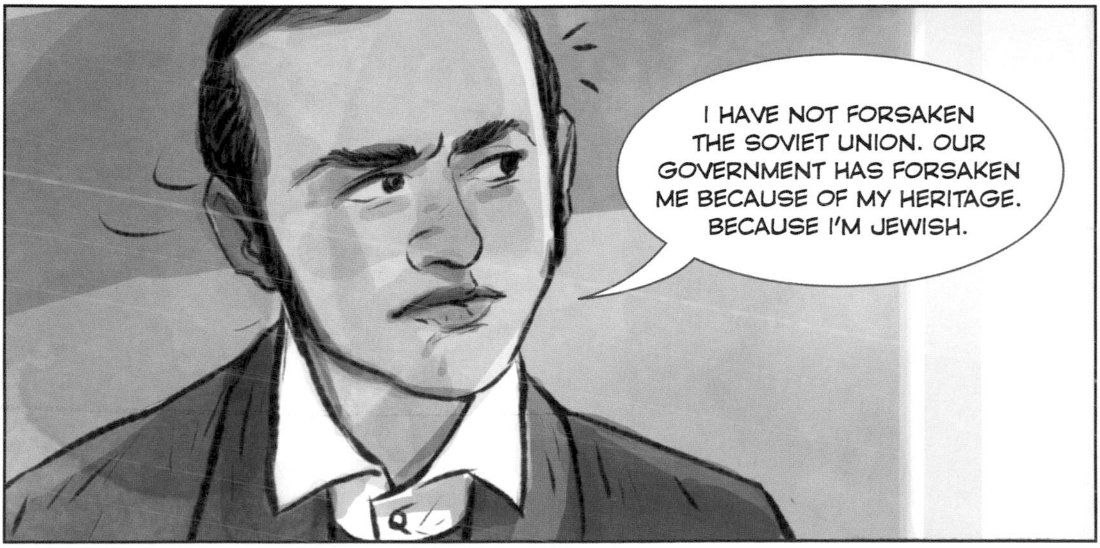
I HAVE NOT FORSAKEN THE SOVIET UNION. OUR GOVERNMENT HAS FORSAKEN ME BECAUSE OF MY HERITAGE. BECAUSE I'M JEWISH.

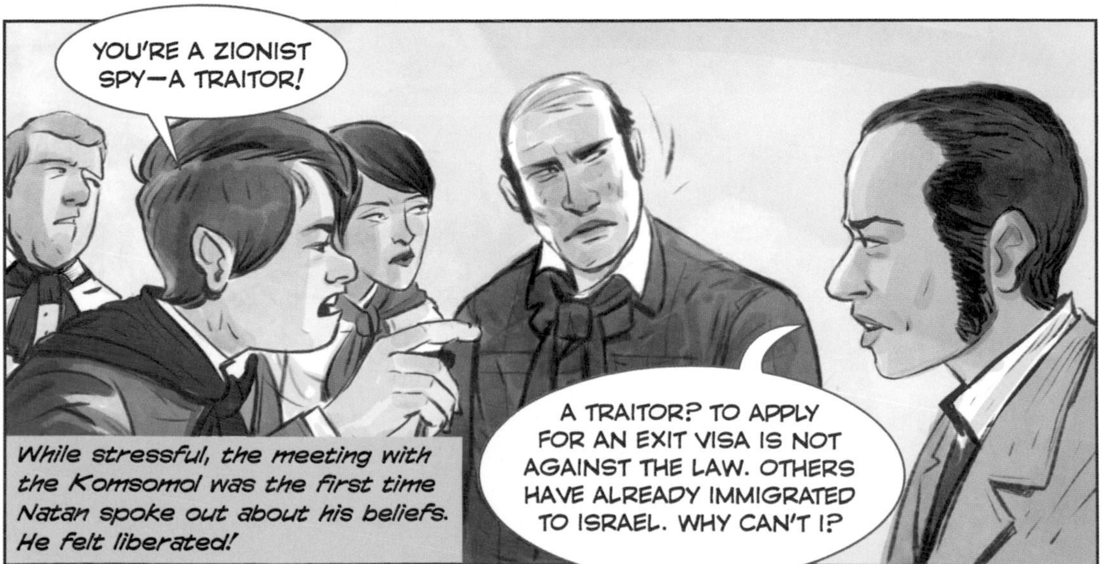
YOU'RE A ZIONIST SPY—A TRAITOR!
While stressful, the meeting with the Komsomol was the first time Natan spoke out about his beliefs. He felt liberated!
A TRAITOR? TO APPLY FOR AN EXIT VISA IS NOT AGAINST THE LAW. OTHERS HAVE ALREADY IMMIGRATED TO ISRAEL. WHY CAN'T I?

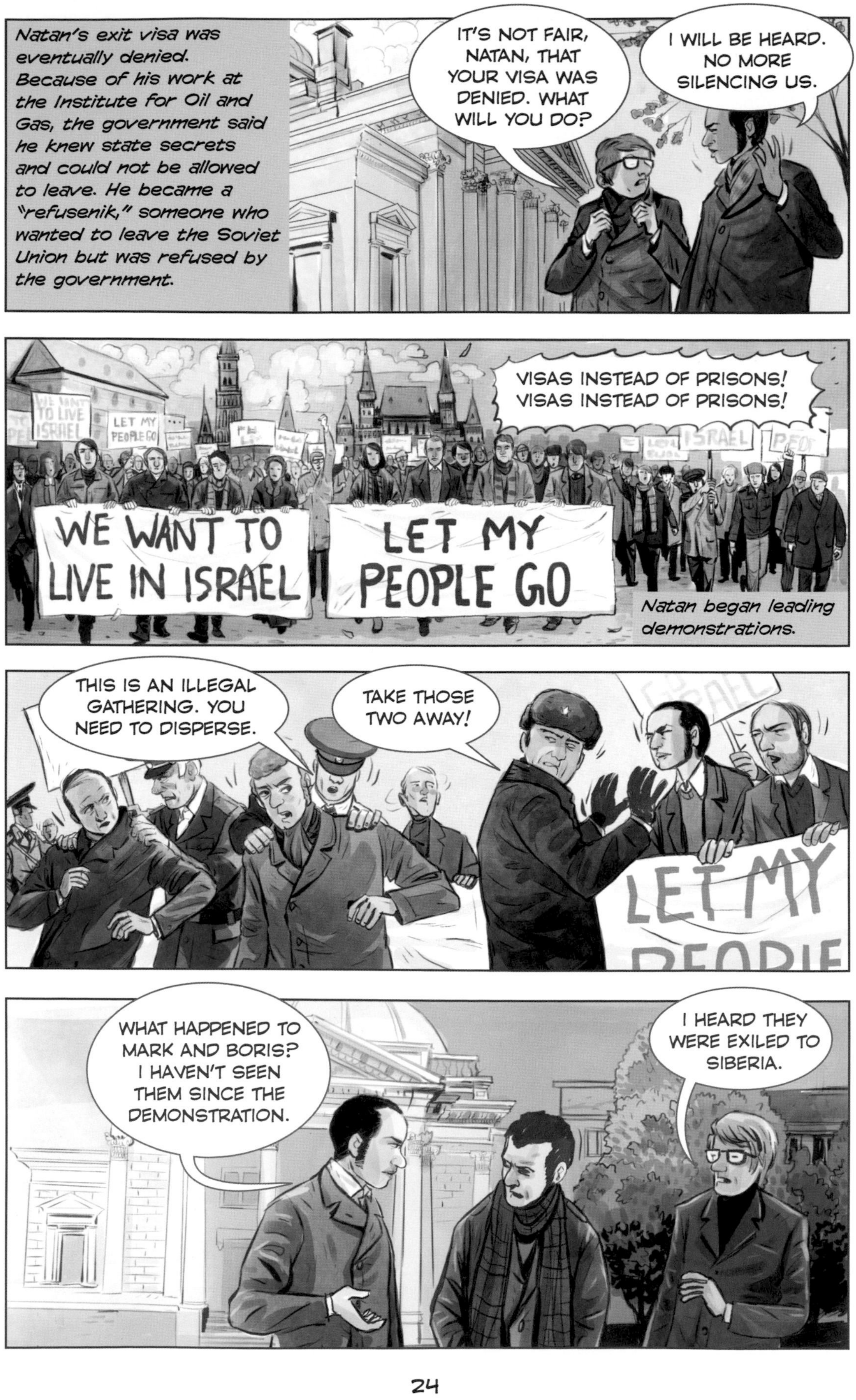
Natan's exit visa was eventually denied. Because of his work at the Institute for Oil and Gas, the government said he knew state secrets and could not be allowed to leave. He became a "refusenik," someone who wanted to leave the Soviet Union but was refused by the government.
IT'S NOT FAIR, NATAN, THAT YOUR VISA WAS DENIED. WHAT WILL YOU DO?
I WILL BE HEARD. NO MORE SILENCING US.
VISAS INSTEAD OF PRISONS! VISAS INSTEAD OF PRISONS!
WE WANT TO LIVE IN ISRAEL
LET MY PEOPLE GO
Natan began leading demonstrations.
THIS IS AN ILLEGAL GATHERING. YOU NEED TO DISPERSE.
TAKE THOSE TWO AWAY!
LET MY
WHAT HAPPENED TO MARK AND BORIS? I HAVEN'T SEEN THEM SINCE THE DEMONSTRATION.
I HEARD THEY WERE EXILED TO SIBERIA.

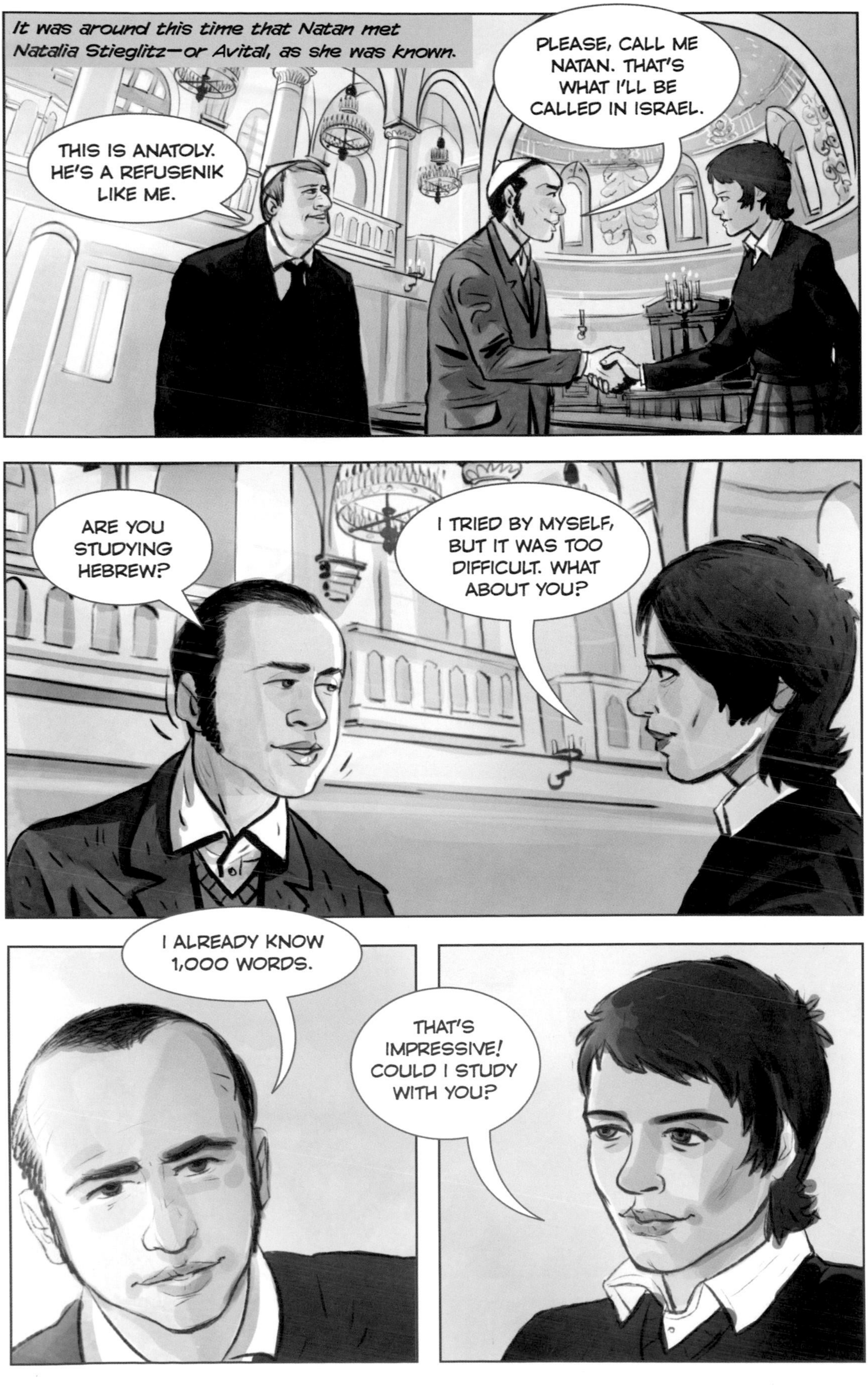
It was around this time that Natan met Natalia Stieglitz—or Avital, as she was known.
THIS IS ANATOLY. HE'S A REFUSENIK LIKE ME.
PLEASE, CALL ME NATAN. THAT'S WHAT I'LL BE CALLED IN ISRAEL.
ARE YOU STUDYING HEBREW?
I TRIED BY MYSELF, BUT IT WAS TOO DIFFICULT. WHAT ABOUT YOU?
I ALREADY KNOW 1,000 WORDS.
THAT'S IMPRESSIVE! COULD I STUDY WITH YOU?

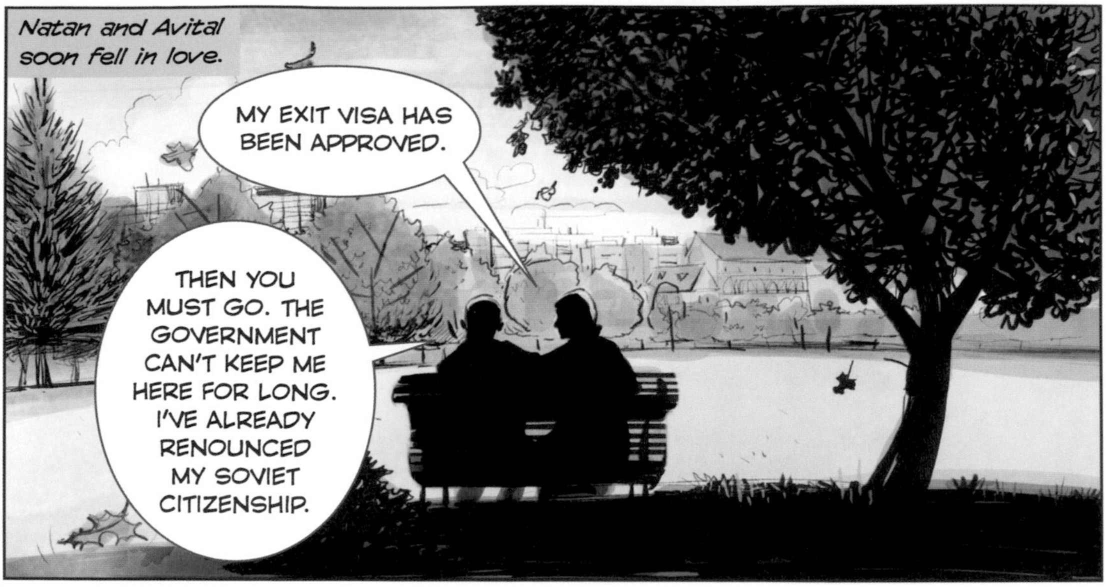
Natan and Avital soon fell in love.
MY EXIT VISA HAS BEEN APPROVED.
THEN YOU MUST GO. THE GOVERNMENT CAN'T KEEP ME HERE FOR LONG. I'VE ALREADY RENOUNCED MY SOVIET CITIZENSHIP.

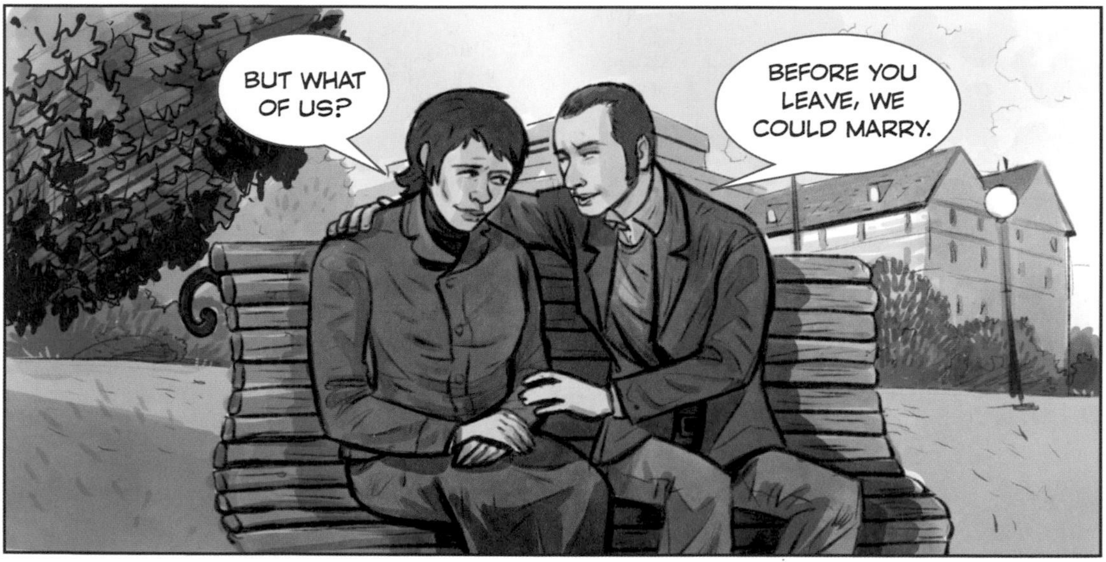
BUT WHAT OF US?
BEFORE YOU LEAVE, WE COULD MARRY.

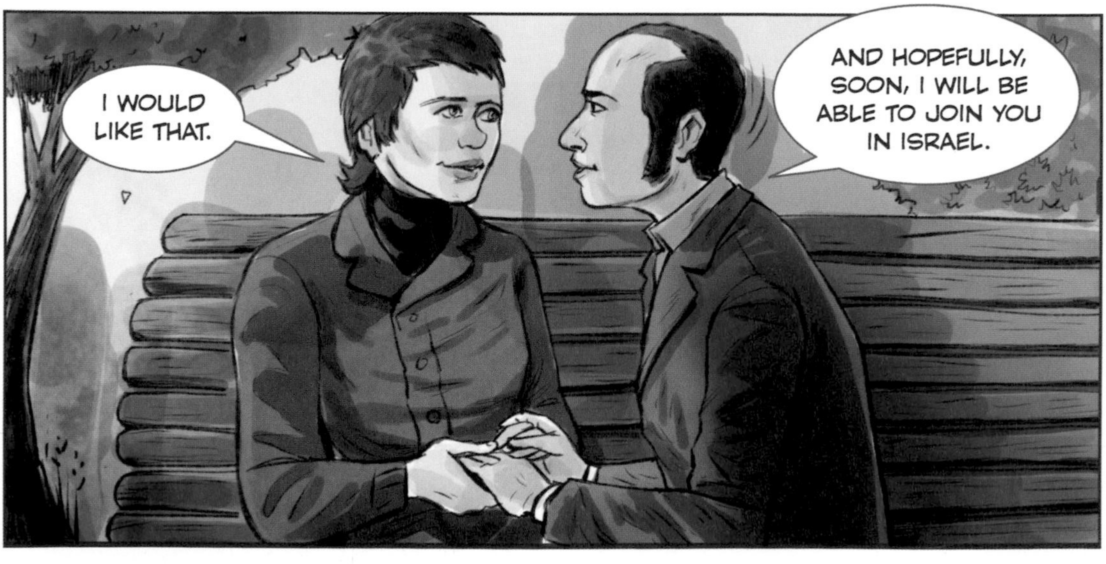
I WOULD LIKE THAT.
AND HOPEFULLY, SOON, I WILL BE ABLE TO JOIN YOU IN ISRAEL.

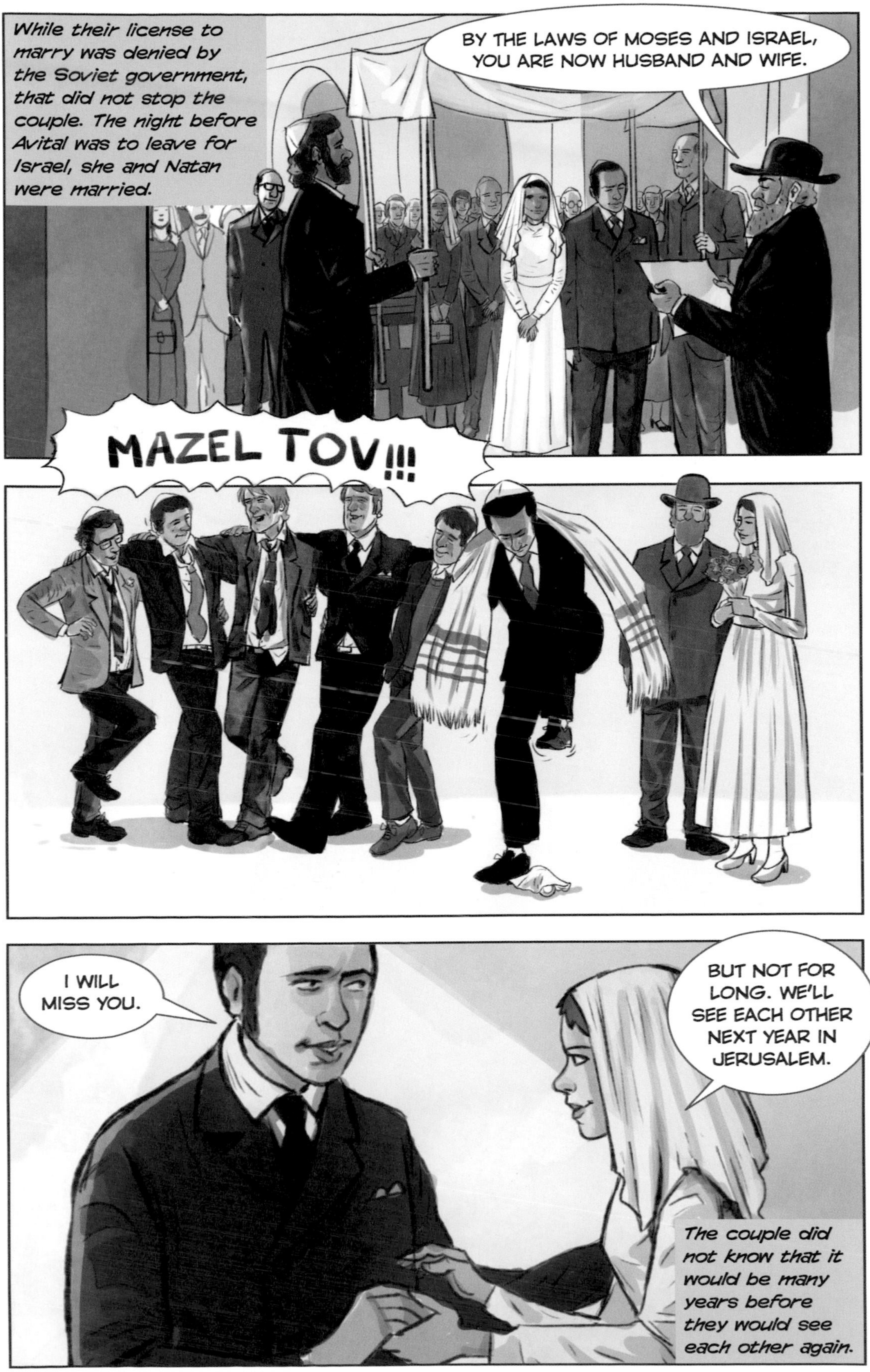
While their license to marry was denied by the Soviet government, that did not stop the couple. The night before Avital was to leave for Israel, she and Natan were married.
BY THE LAWS OF MOSES AND ISRAEL, YOU ARE NOW HUSBAND AND WIFE.
MAZEL TOV!!!
I WILL MISS YOU.
BUT NOT FOR LONG. WE'LL SEE EACH OTHER NEXT YEAR IN JERUSALEM.
The couple did not know that it would be many years before they would see each other again.

3 ARREST!

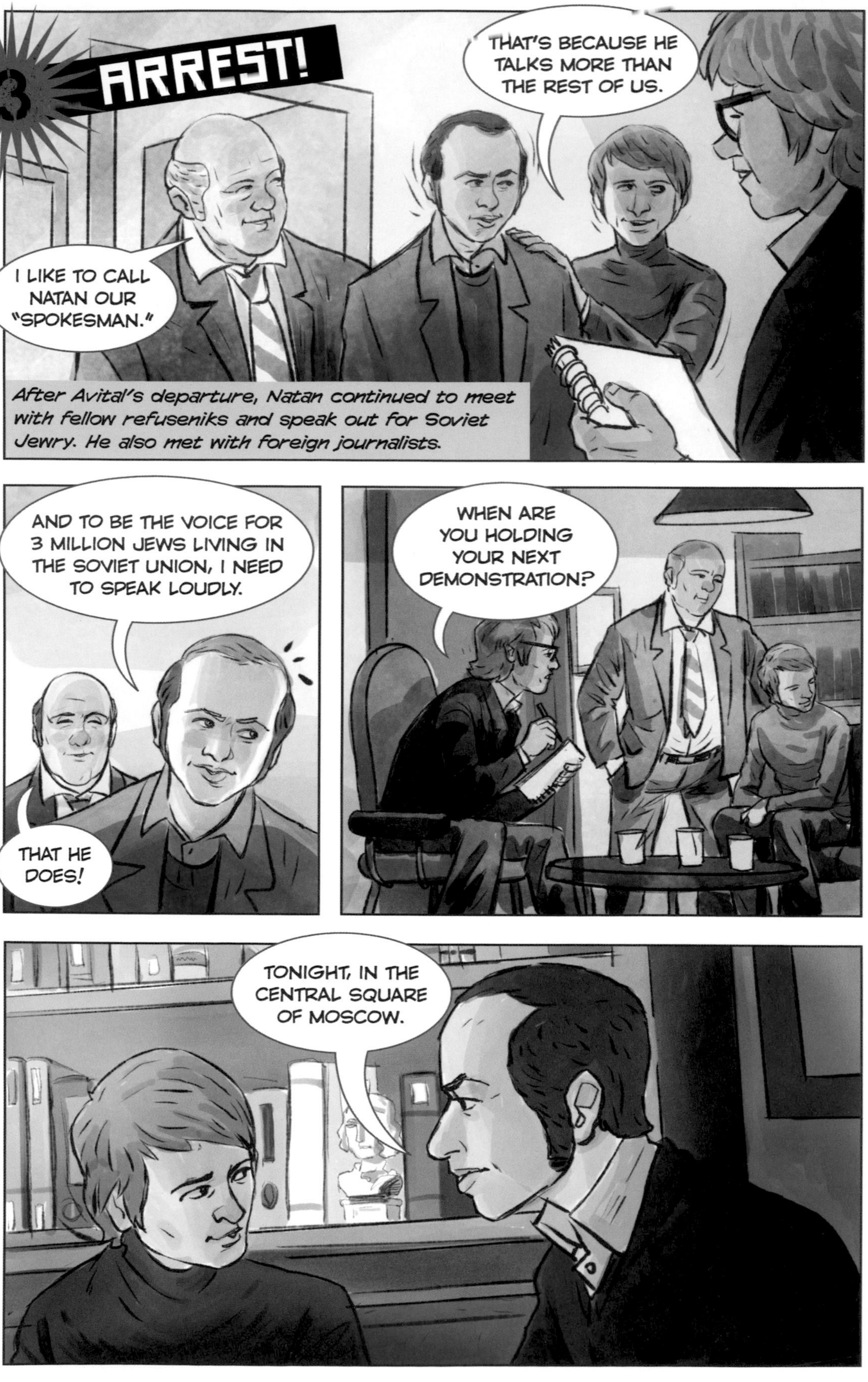
After Avital's departure, Natan continued to meet with fellow refuseniks and speak out for Soviet Jewry. He also met with foreign journalists.
I LIKE TO CALL NATAN OUR "SPOKESMAN."
THAT'S BECAUSE HE TALKS MORE THAN THE REST OF US.
AND TO BE THE VOICE FOR 3 MILLION JEWS LIVING IN THE SOVIET UNION, I NEED TO SPEAK LOUDLY.
THAT HE DOES!
WHEN ARE YOU HOLDING YOUR NEXT DEMONSTRATION?
TONIGHT, IN THE CENTRAL SQUARE OF MOSCOW.

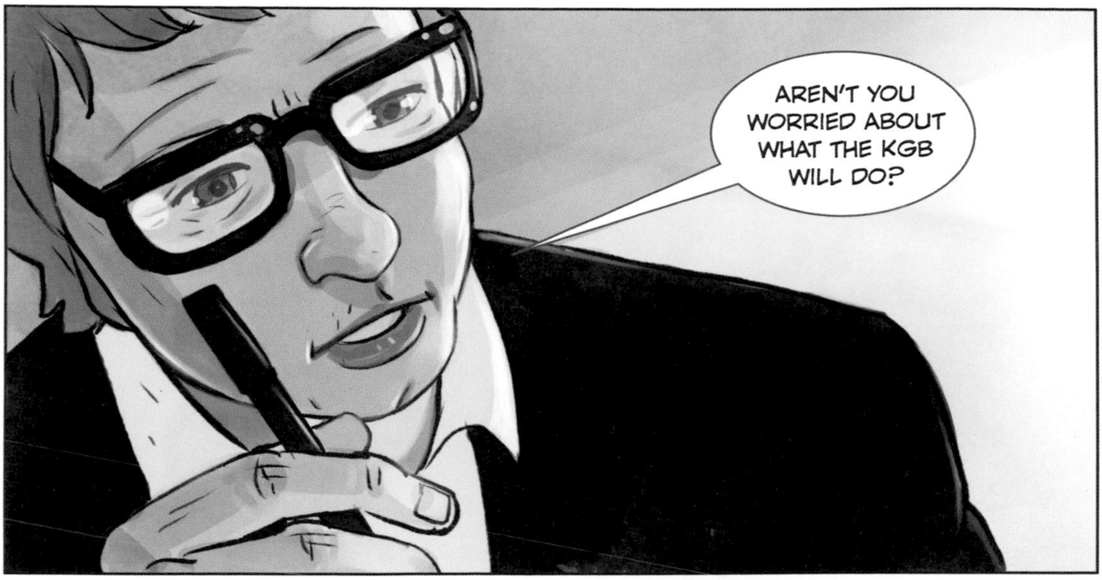
AREN'T YOU WORRIED ABOUT WHAT THE KGB WILL DO?

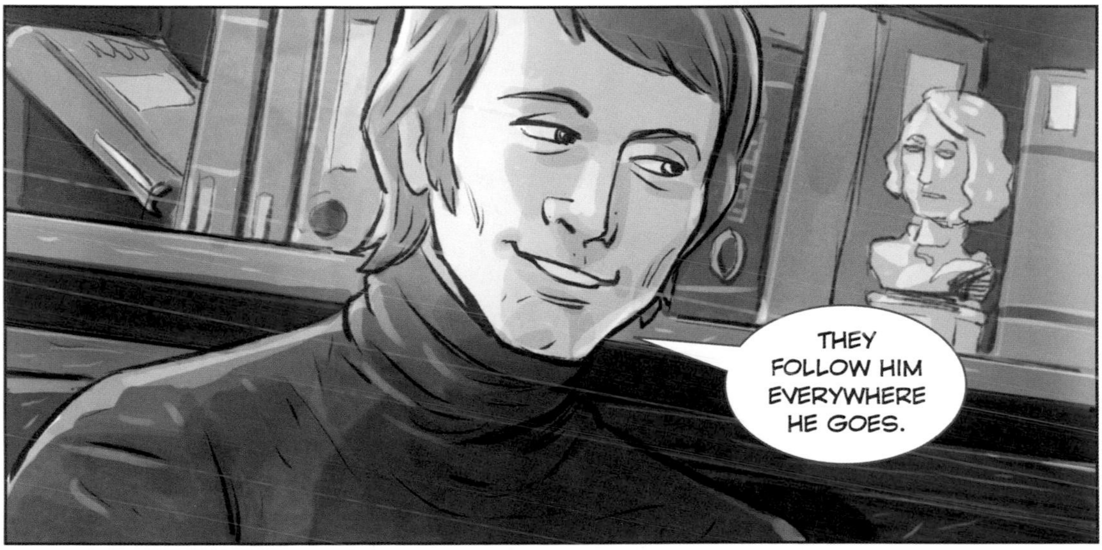
THEY FOLLOW HIM EVERYWHERE HE GOES.

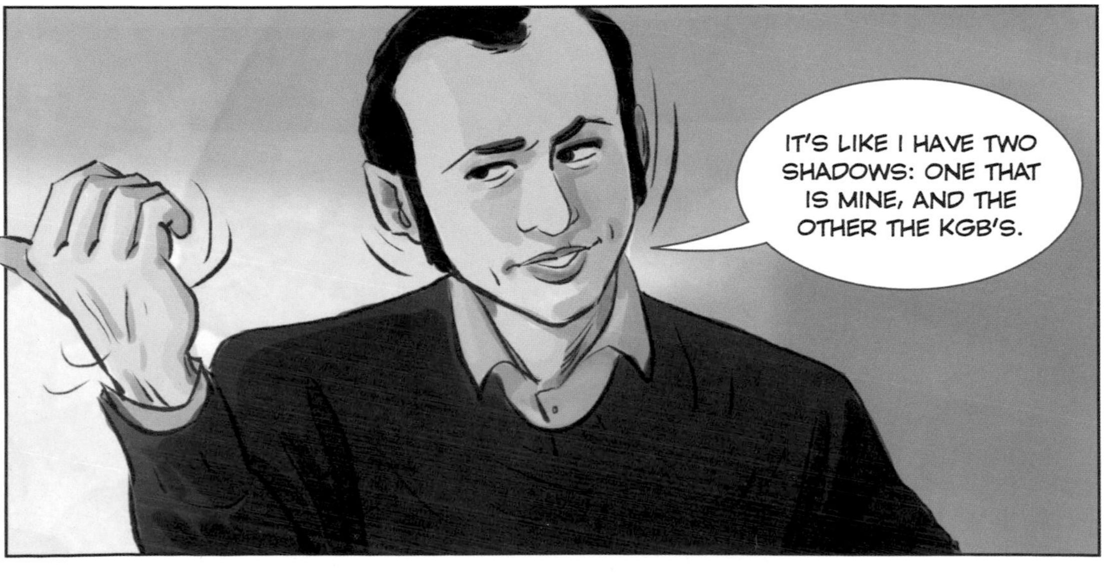
IT'S LIKE I HAVE TWO SHADOWS: ONE THAT IS MINE, AND THE OTHER THE KGB'S.

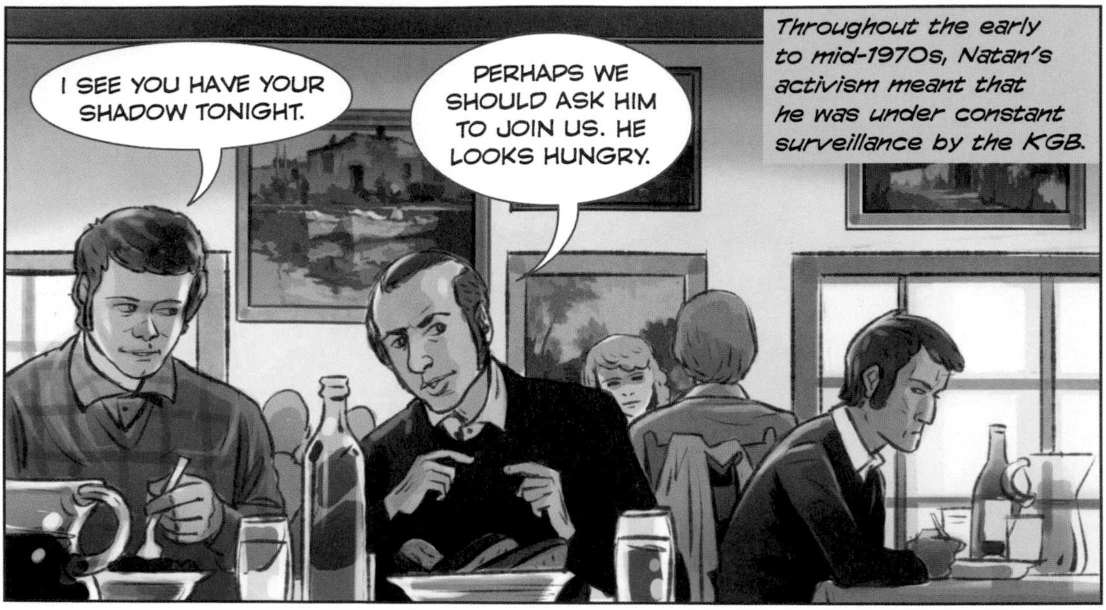
Throughout the early to mid-1970s, Natan's activism meant that he was under constant surveillance by the KGB.
I SEE YOU HAVE YOUR SHADOW TONIGHT.
PERHAPS WE SHOULD ASK HIM TO JOIN US. HE LOOKS HUNGRY.

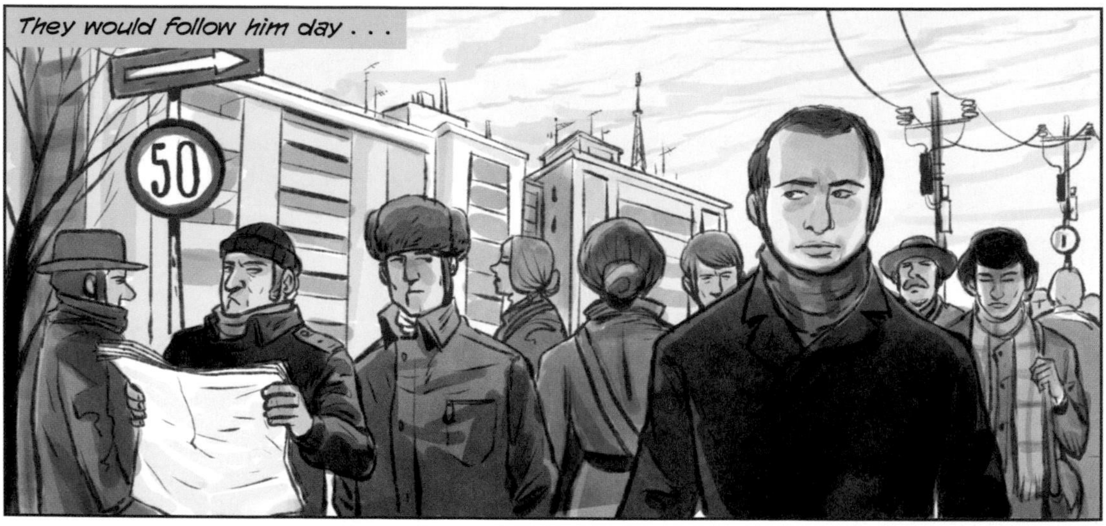
They would follow him day . . .
50

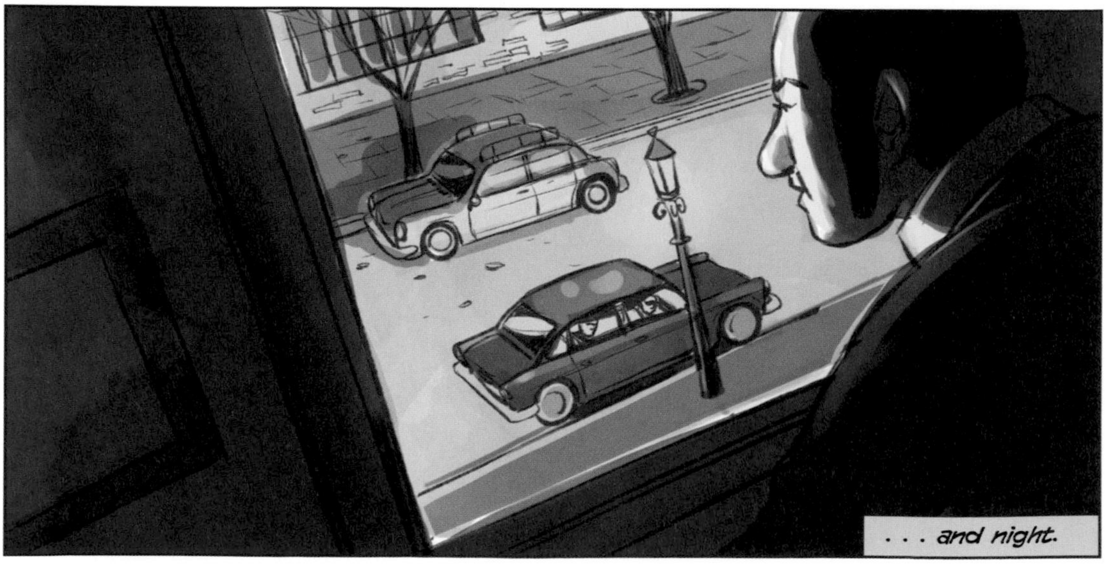
. . . and night.

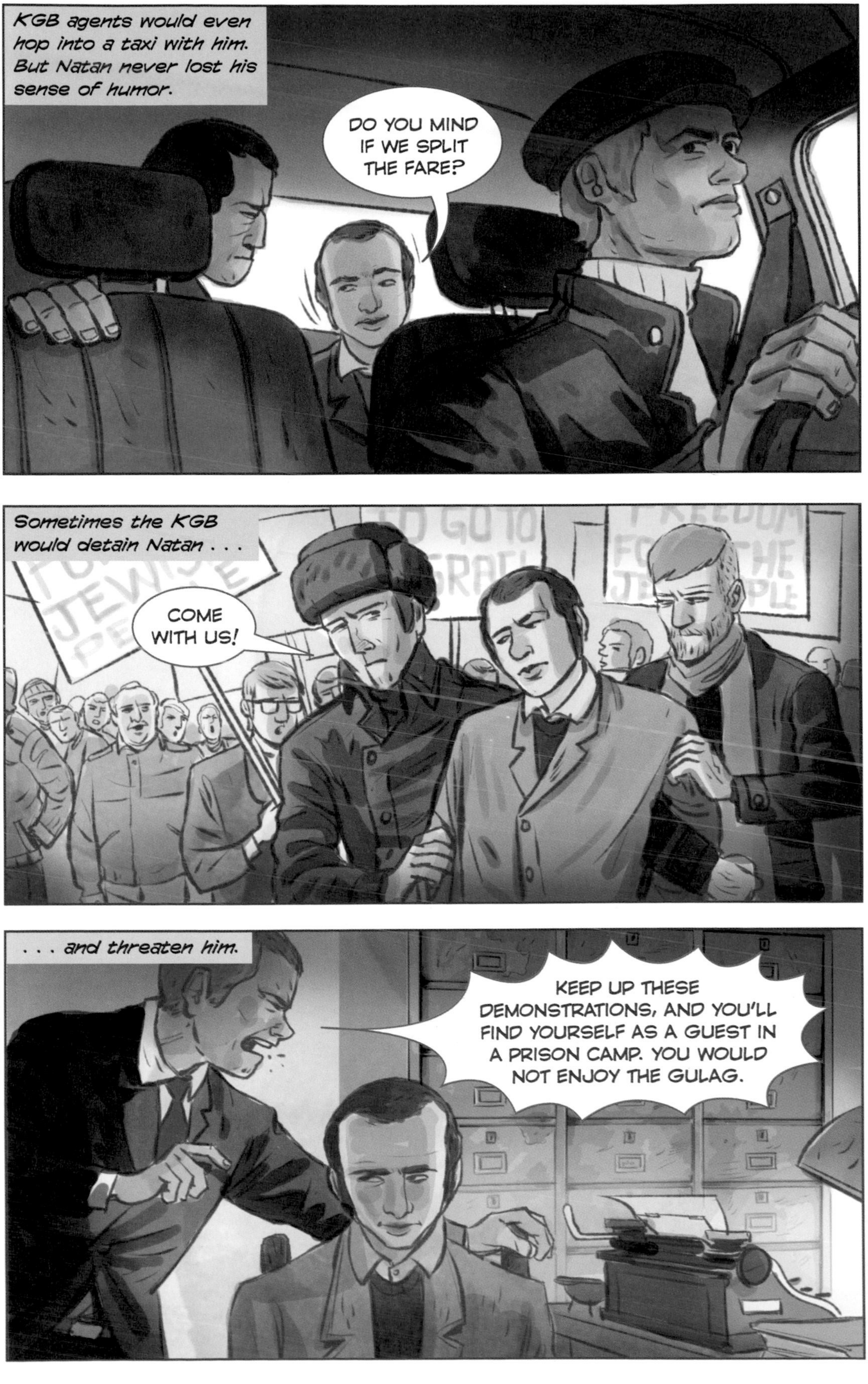
KGB agents would even hop into a taxi with him. But Natan never lost his sense of humor.
DO YOU MIND IF WE SPLIT THE FARE?
Sometimes the KGB would detain Natan . . .
COME WITH US!
. . . and threaten him.
KEEP UP THESE DEMONSTRATIONS, AND YOU'LL FIND YOURSELF AS A GUEST IN A PRISON CAMP. YOU WOULD NOT ENJOY THE GULAG.

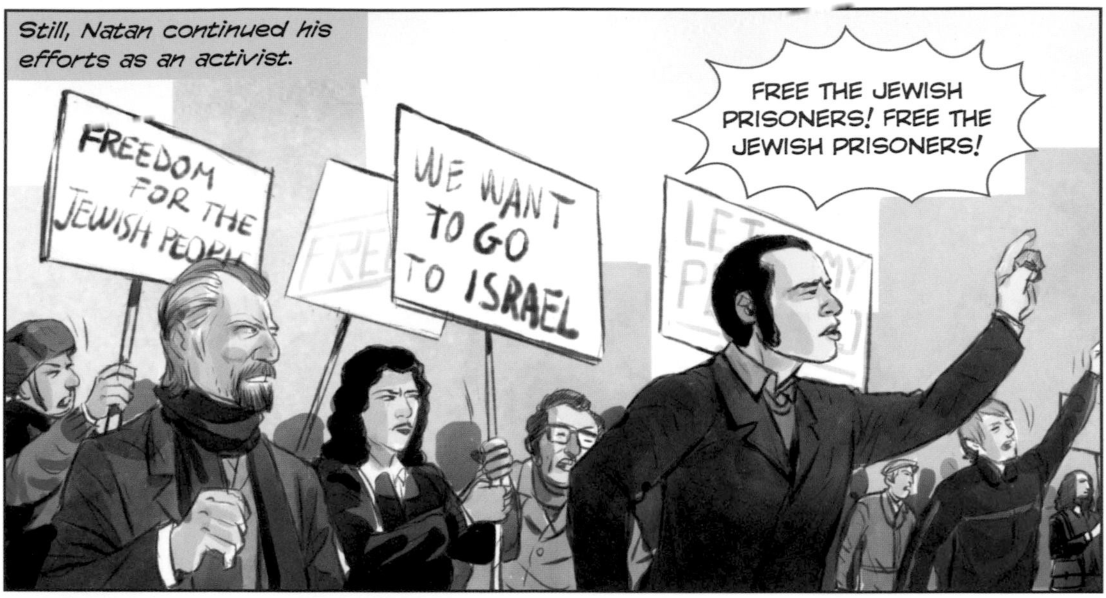
Still, Natan continued his efforts as an activist.
FREE THE JEWISH PRISONERS! FREE THE JEWISH PRISONERS!
FREEDOM FOR THE JEWISH
WE WANT TO GO TO ISRAEL

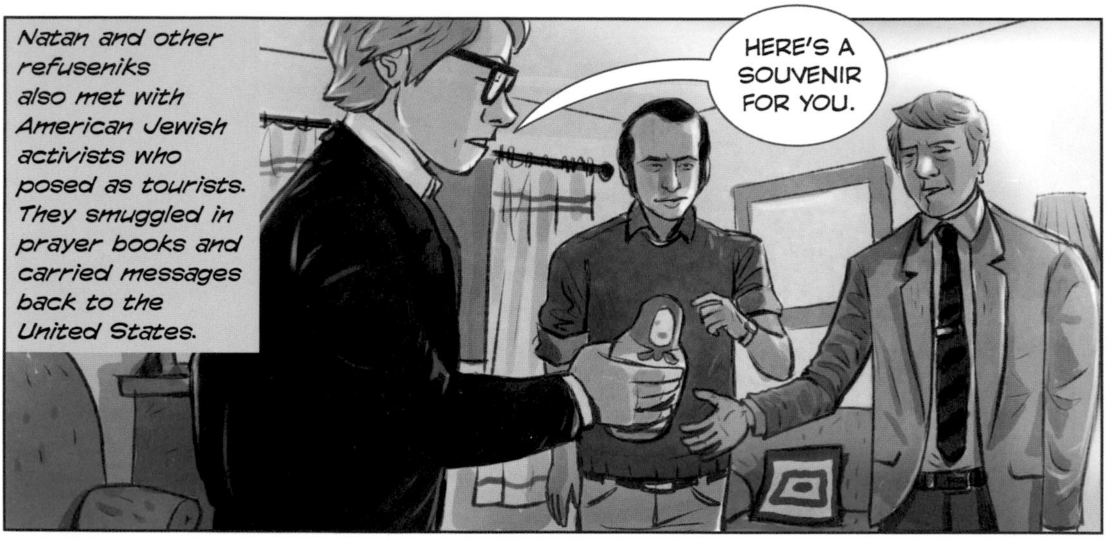
Natan and other refuseniks also met with American Jewish activists who posed as tourists. They smuggled in prayer books and carried messages back to the United States.
HERE'S A SOUVENIR FOR YOU.

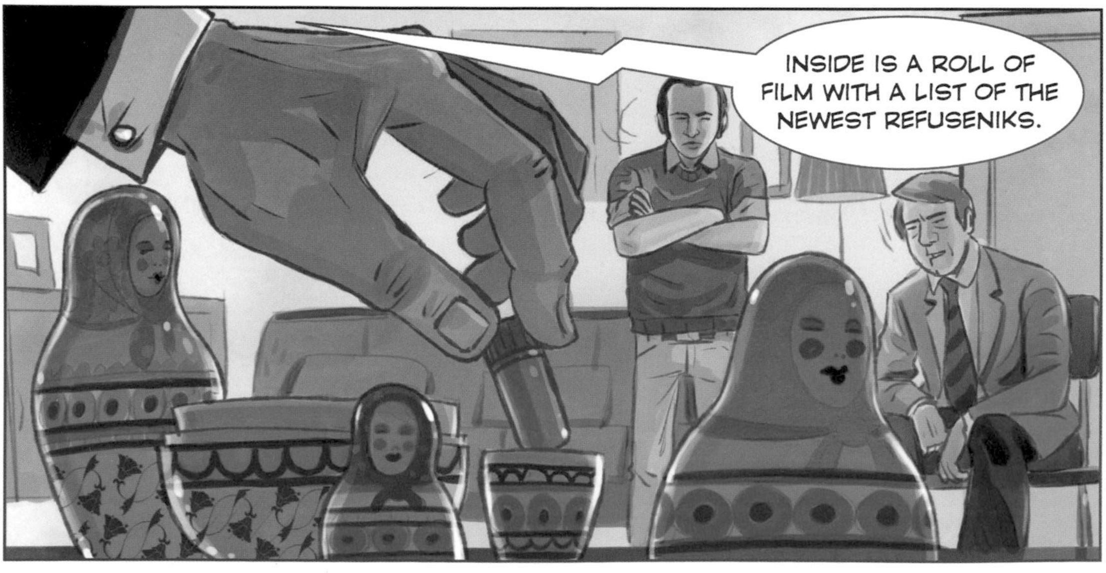
INSIDE IS A ROLL OF FILM WITH A LIST OF THE NEWEST REFUSENIKS.

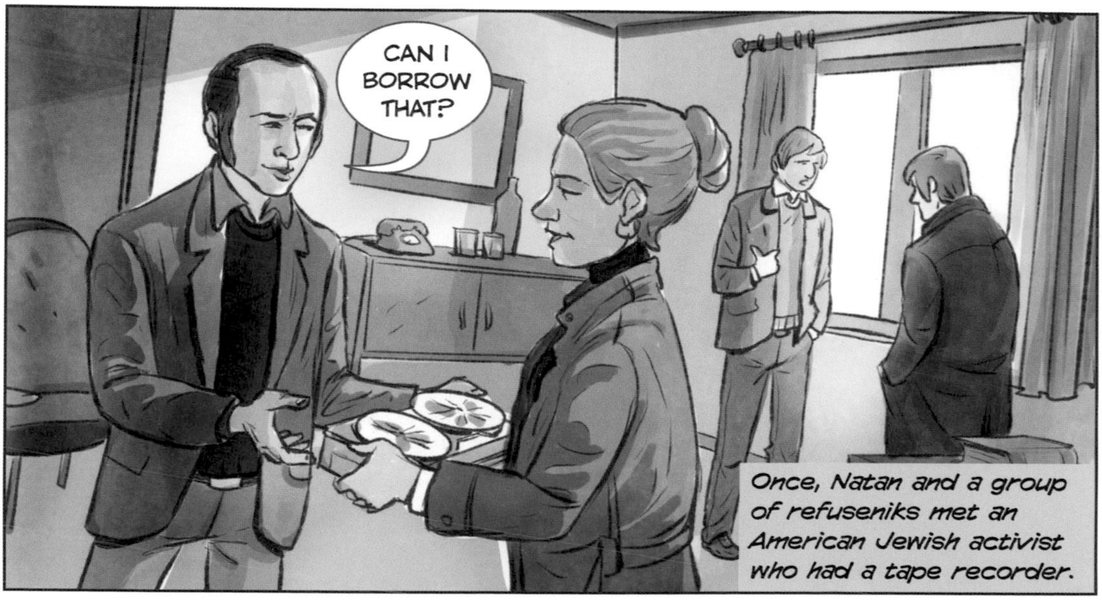
CAN I BORROW THAT?
Once, Natan and a group of refuseniks met an American Jewish activist who had a tape recorder.

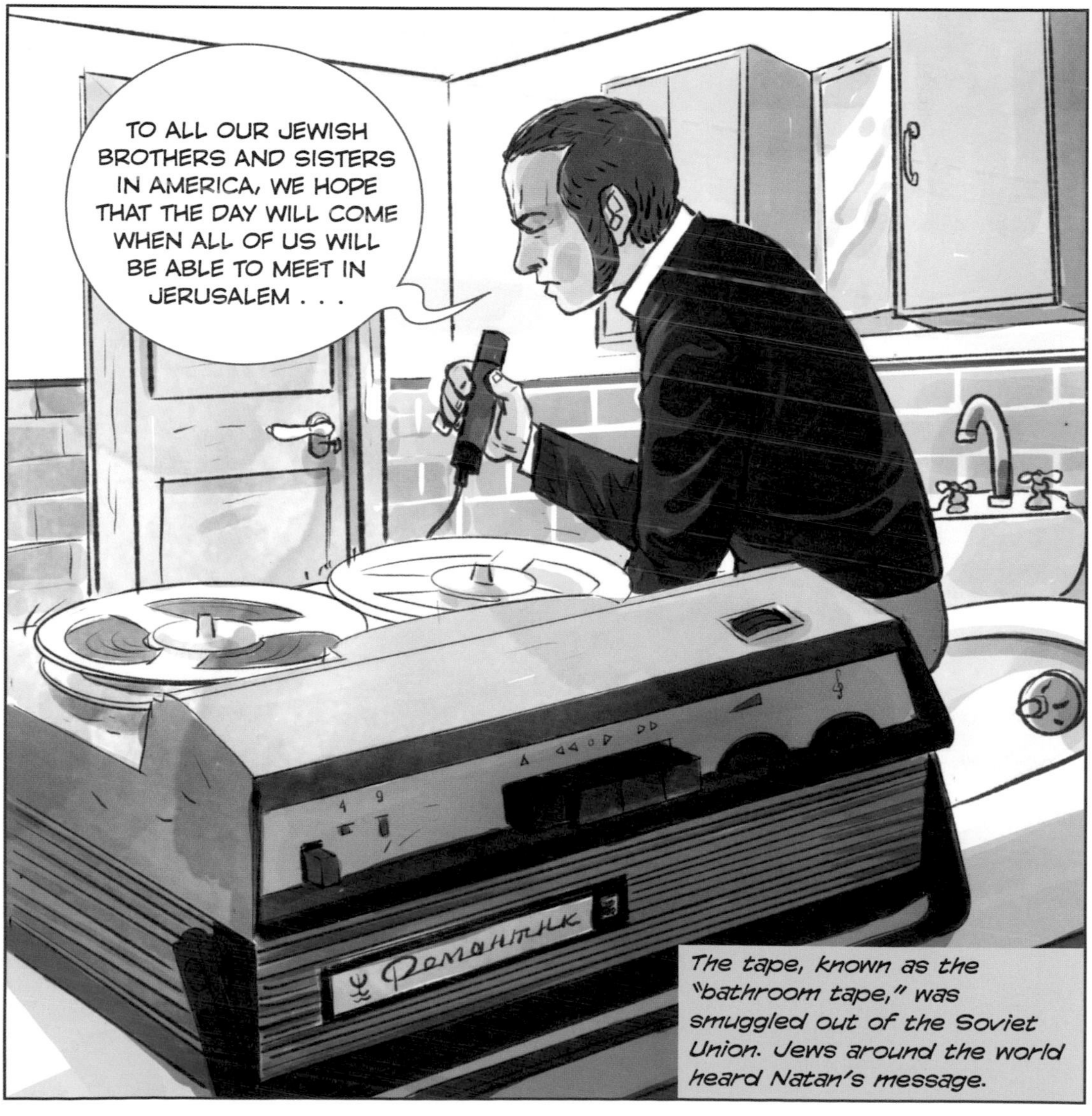
TO ALL OUR JEWISH BROTHERS AND SISTERS IN AMERICA, WE HOPE THAT THE DAY WILL COME WHEN ALL OF US WILL BE ABLE TO MEET IN JERUSALEM . . .
The tape, known as the "bathroom tape," was smuggled out of the Soviet Union. Jews around the world heard Natan's message.

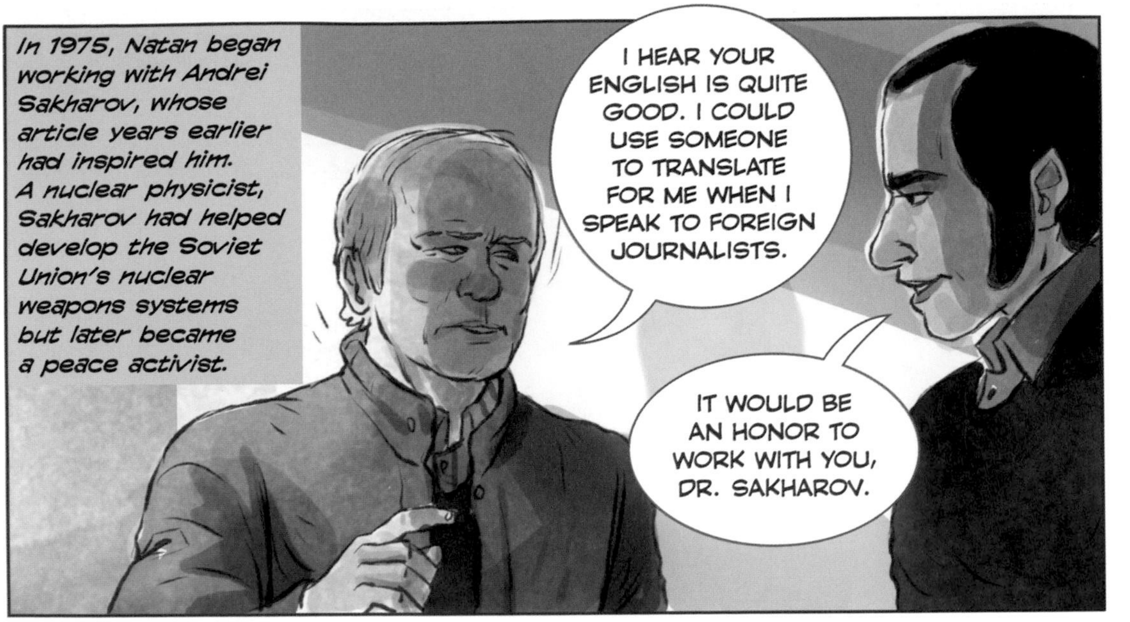
In 1975, Natan began working with Andrei Sakharov, whose article years earlier had inspired him. A nuclear physicist, Sakharov had helped develop the Soviet Union's nuclear weapons systems but later became a peace activist.
I HEAR YOUR ENGLISH IS QUITE GOOD. I COULD USE SOMEONE TO TRANSLATE FOR ME WHEN I SPEAK TO FOREIGN JOURNALISTS.
IT WOULD BE AN HONOR TO WORK WITH YOU, DR. SAKHAROV.

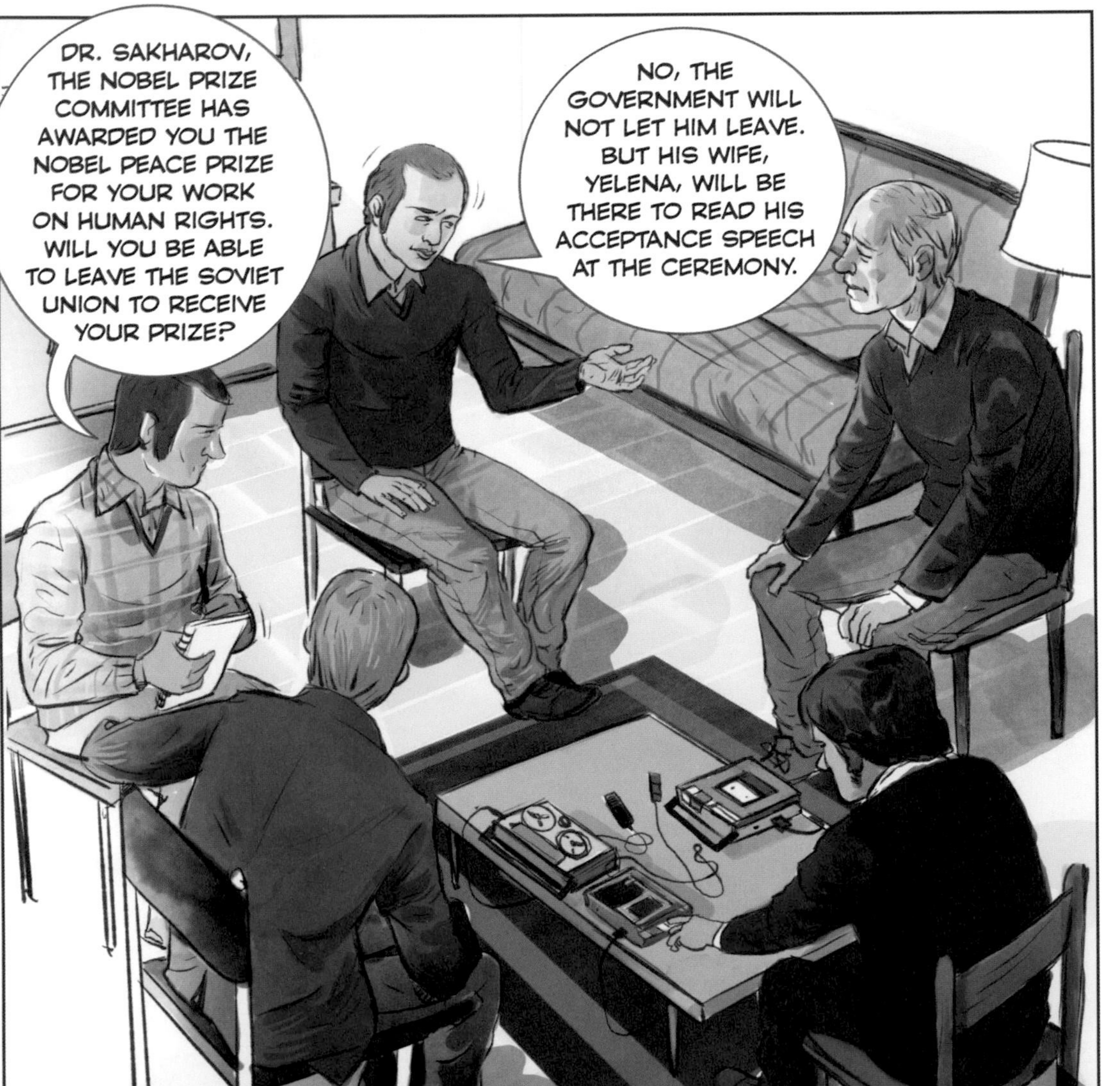
DR. SAKHAROV, THE NOBEL PRIZE COMMITTEE HAS AWARDED YOU THE NOBEL PEACE PRIZE FOR YOUR WORK ON HUMAN RIGHTS. WILL YOU BE ABLE TO LEAVE THE SOVIET UNION TO RECEIVE YOUR PRIZE?
NO, THE GOVERNMENT WILL NOT LET HIM LEAVE. BUT HIS WIFE, YELENA, WILL BE THERE TO READ HIS ACCEPTANCE SPEECH AT THE CEREMONY.

That same year, European countries—including the Soviet Union—along with the United States and Canada signed the Helsinki Accords. These documents were meant to protect human rights and freedom for all peoples.

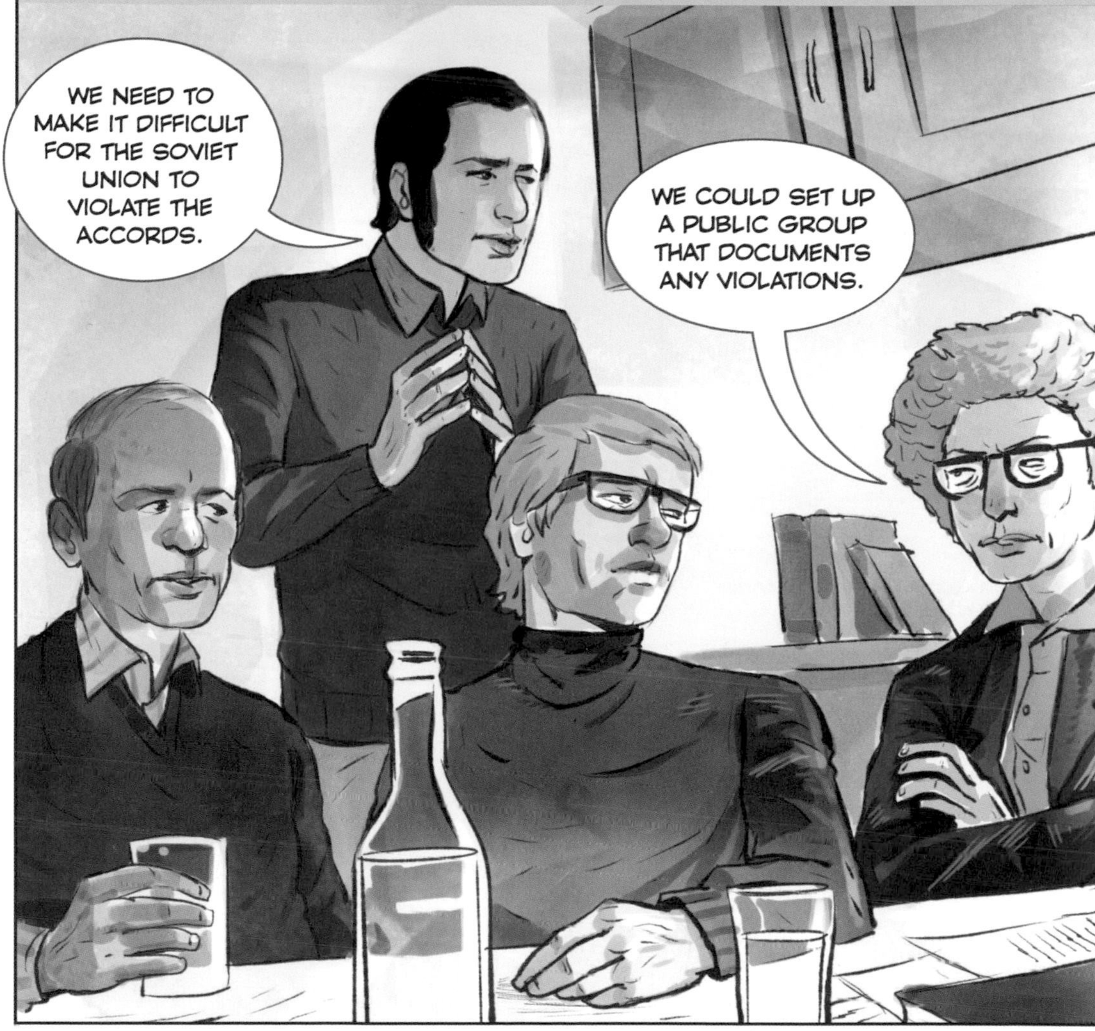
WE NEED TO MAKE IT DIFFICULT FOR THE SOVIET UNION TO VIOLATE THE ACCORDS.
WE COULD SET UP A PUBLIC GROUP THAT DOCUMENTS ANY VIOLATIONS.

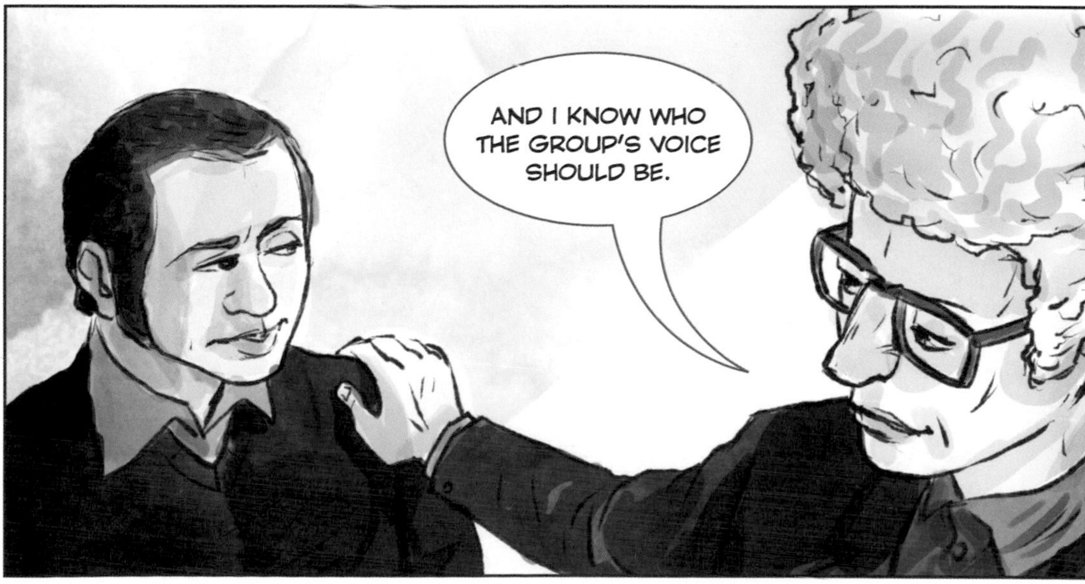
AND I KNOW WHO THE GROUP'S VOICE SHOULD BE.

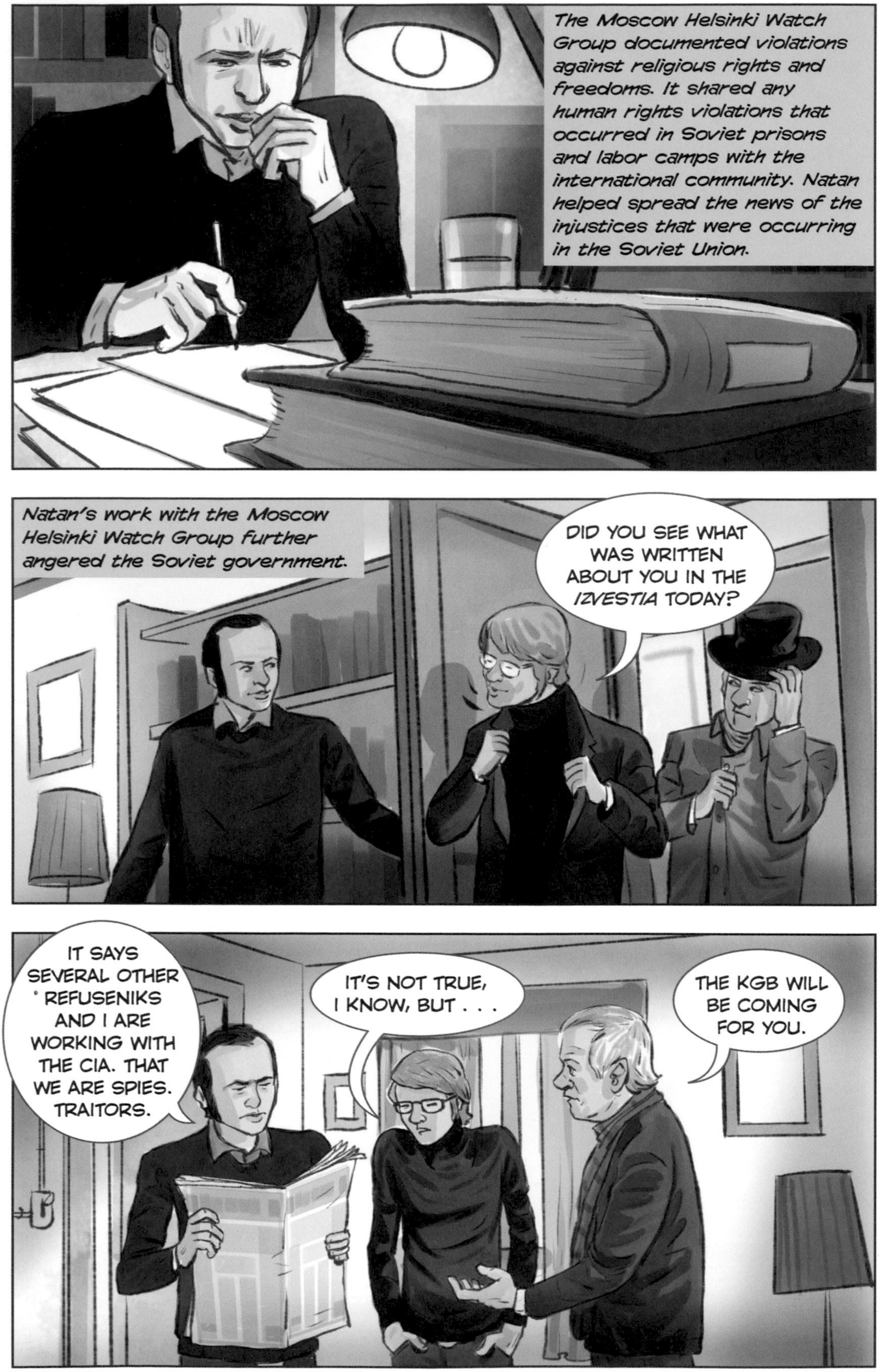
The Moscow Helsinki Watch Group documented violations against religious rights and freedoms. It shared any human rights violations that occurred in Soviet prisons and labor camps with the international community. Natan helped spread the news of the injustices that were occurring in the Soviet Union.
Natan's work with the Moscow Helsinki Watch Group further angered the Soviet government.
DID YOU SEE WHAT WAS WRITTEN ABOUT YOU IN THE *IZVESTIA* TODAY?
IT SAYS SEVERAL OTHER REFUSENIKS AND I ARE WORKING WITH THE CIA. THAT WE ARE SPIES. TRAITORS.
IT'S NOT TRUE, I KNOW, BUT . . .
THE KGB WILL BE COMING FOR YOU.

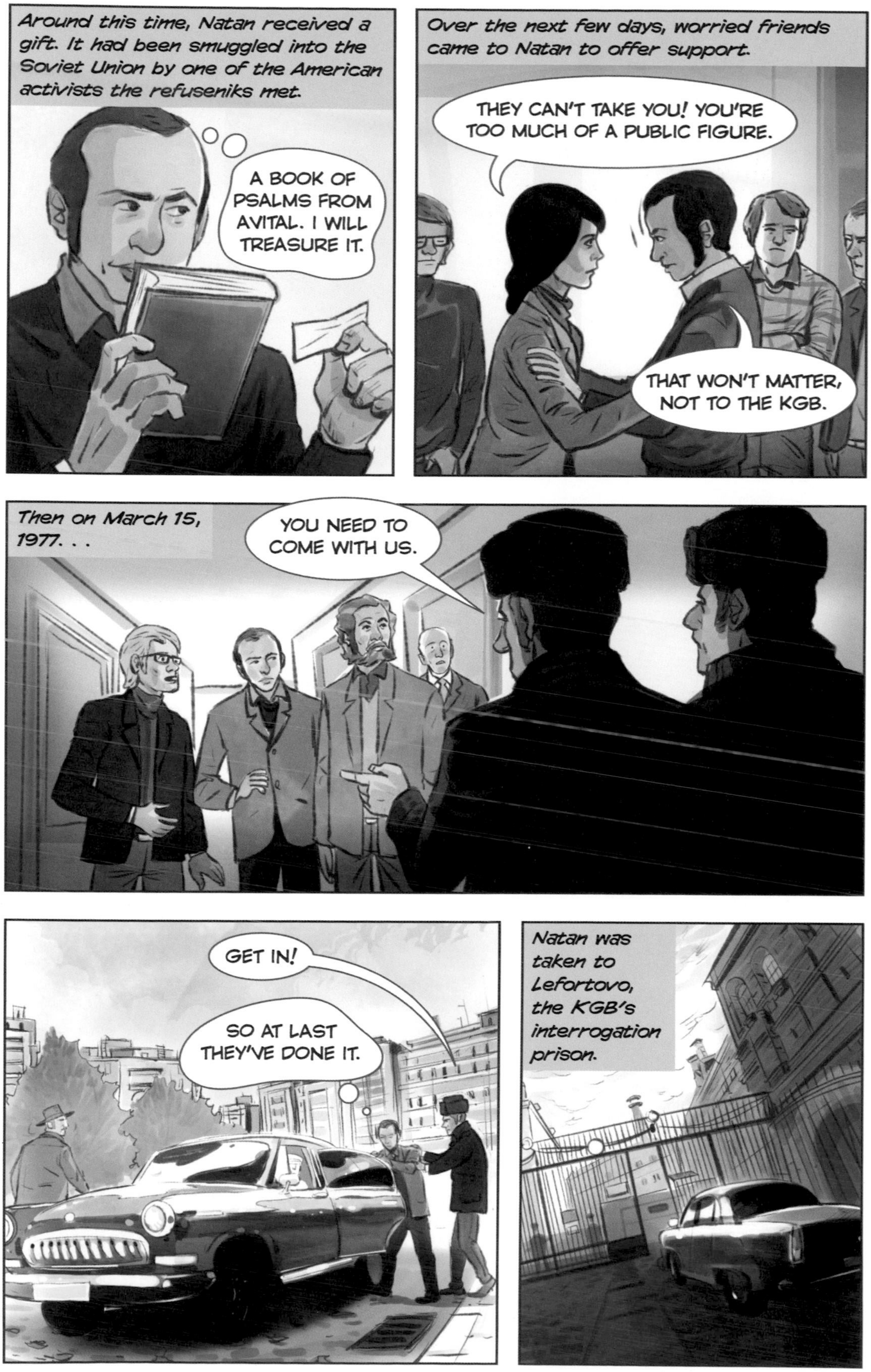
Around this time, Natan received a gift. It had been smuggled into the Soviet Union by one of the American activists the refuseniks met.
A BOOK OF PSALMS FROM AVITAL. I WILL TREASURE IT.
Over the next few days, worried friends came to Natan to offer support.
THEY CAN'T TAKE YOU! YOU'RE TOO MUCH OF A PUBLIC FIGURE.
THAT WON'T MATTER, NOT TO THE KGB.
Then on March 15, 1977. . .
YOU NEED TO COME WITH US.
GET IN!
SO AT LAST THEY'VE DONE IT.
Natan was taken to Lefortovo, the KGB's interrogation prison.

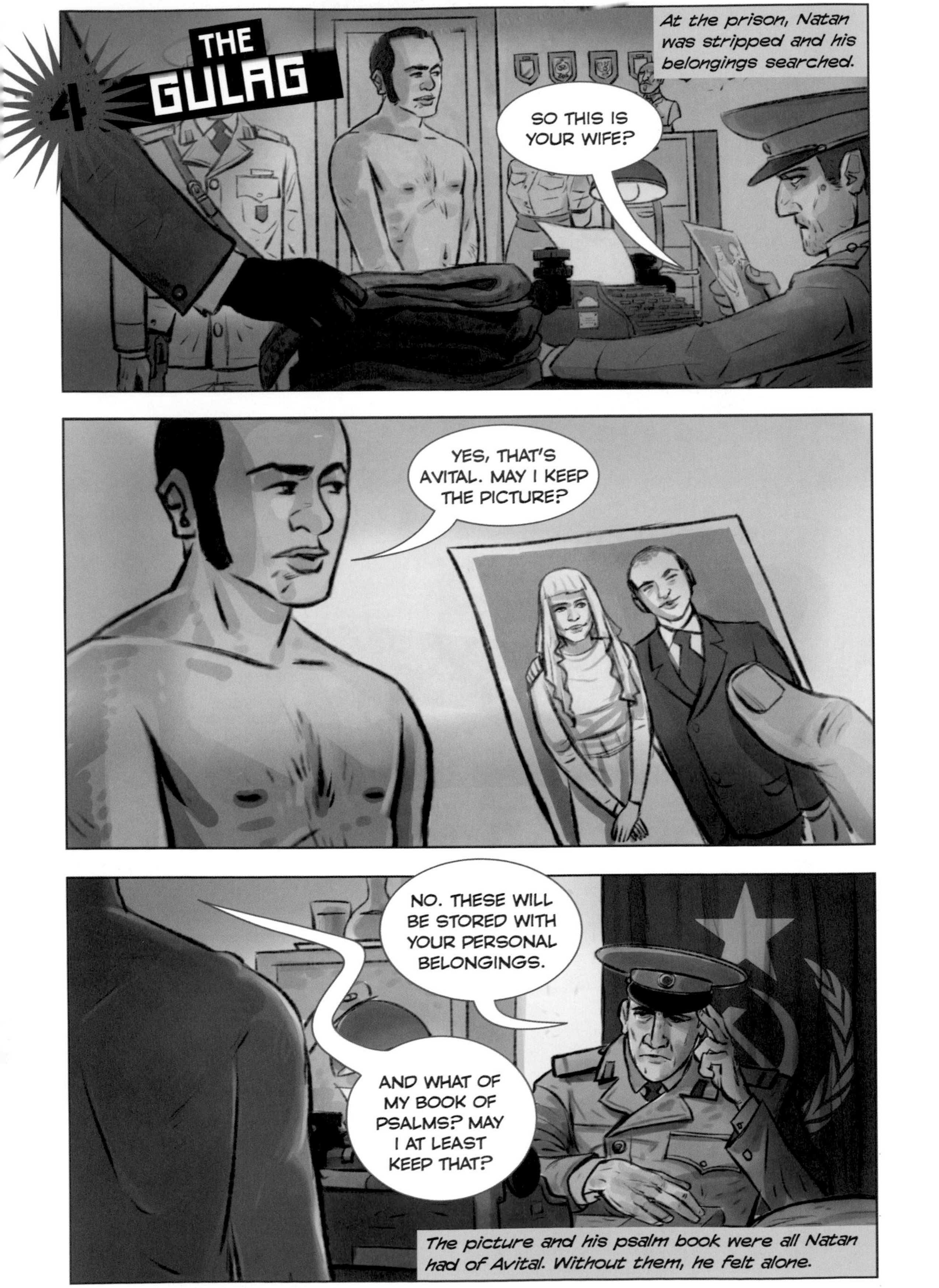
4
THE GULAG
At the prison, Natan was stripped and his belongings searched.
SO THIS IS YOUR WIFE?
YES, THAT'S AVITAL. MAY I KEEP THE PICTURE?
NO. THESE WILL BE STORED WITH YOUR PERSONAL BELONGINGS.
AND WHAT OF MY BOOK OF PSALMS? MAY I AT LEAST KEEP THAT?
The picture and his psalm book were all Natan had of Avital. Without them, he felt alone.

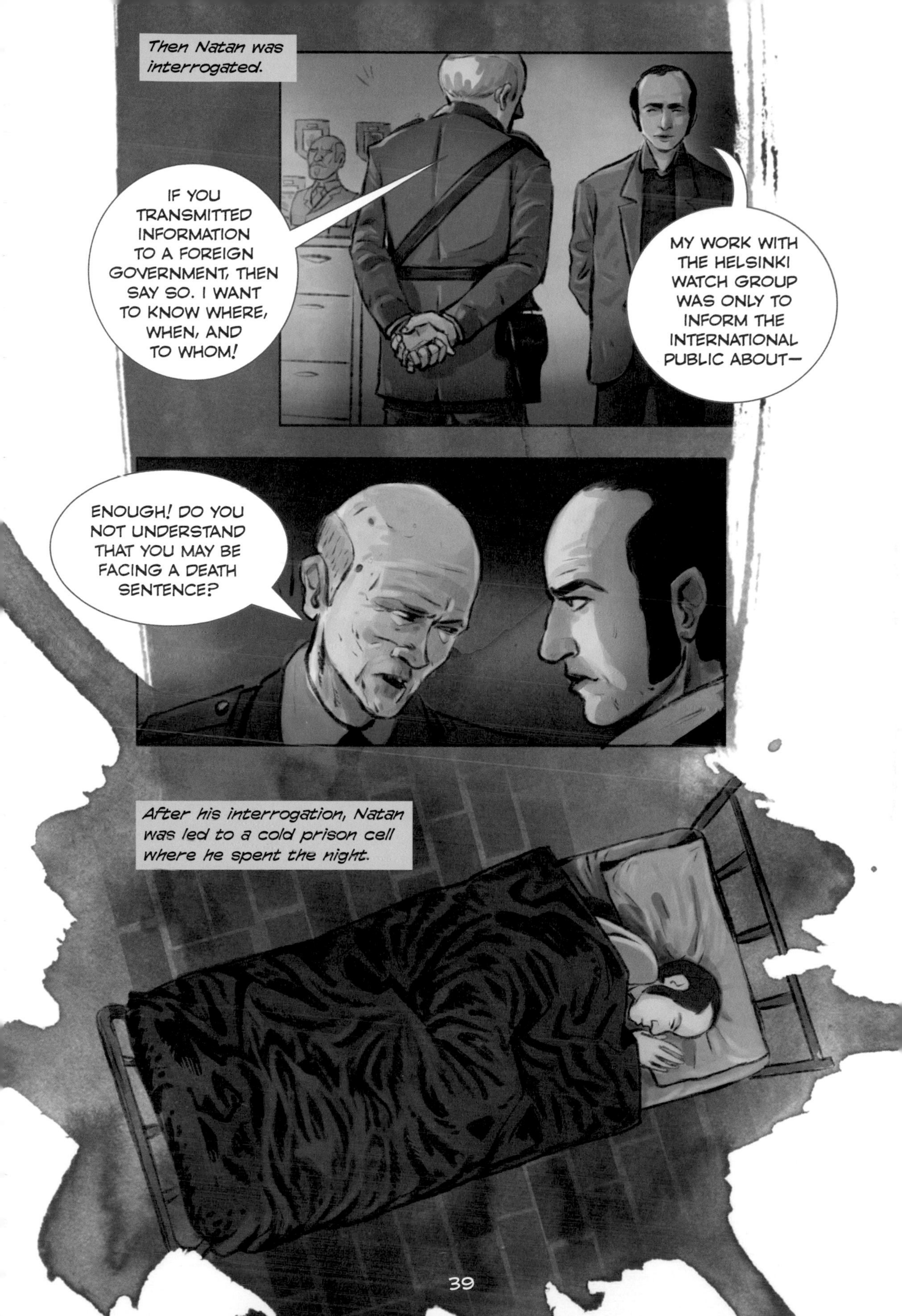
Then Natan was interrogated.
IF YOU TRANSMITTED INFORMATION TO A FOREIGN GOVERNMENT, THEN SAY SO. I WANT TO KNOW WHERE, WHEN, AND TO WHOM!
MY WORK WITH THE HELSINKI WATCH GROUP WAS ONLY TO INFORM THE INTERNATIONAL PUBLIC ABOUT—
ENOUGH! DO YOU NOT UNDERSTAND THAT YOU MAY BE FACING A DEATH SENTENCE?
After his interrogation, Natan was led to a cold prison cell where he spent the night.

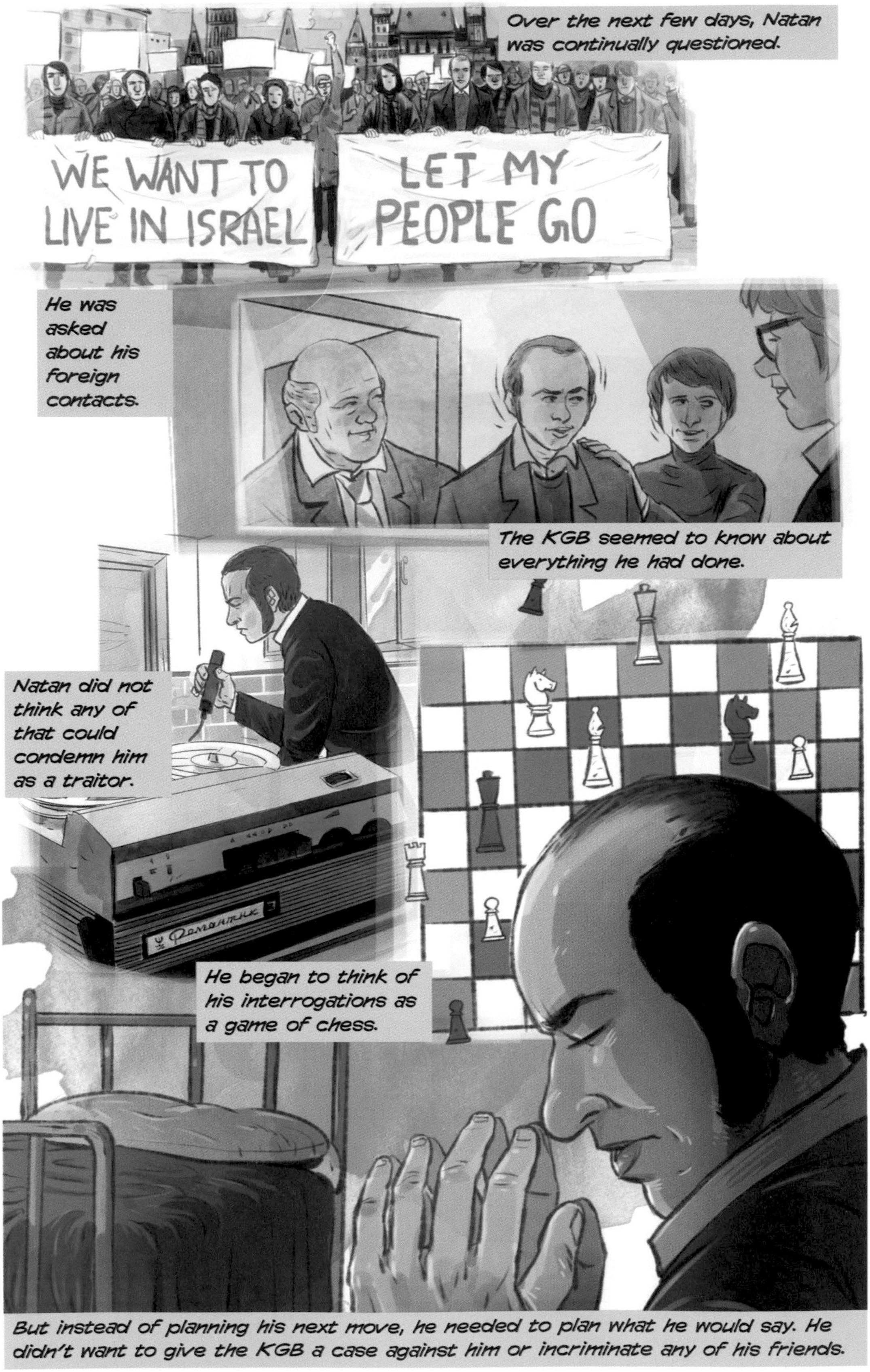
Over the next few days, Natan was continually questioned.
WE WANT TO LIVE IN ISRAEL
LET MY PEOPLE GO
He was asked about his foreign contacts.
The KGB seemed to know about everything he had done.
Natan did not think any of that could condemn him as a traitor.
He began to think of his interrogations as a game of chess.
But instead of planning his next move, he needed to plan what he would say. He didn't want to give the KGB a case against him or incriminate any of his friends.

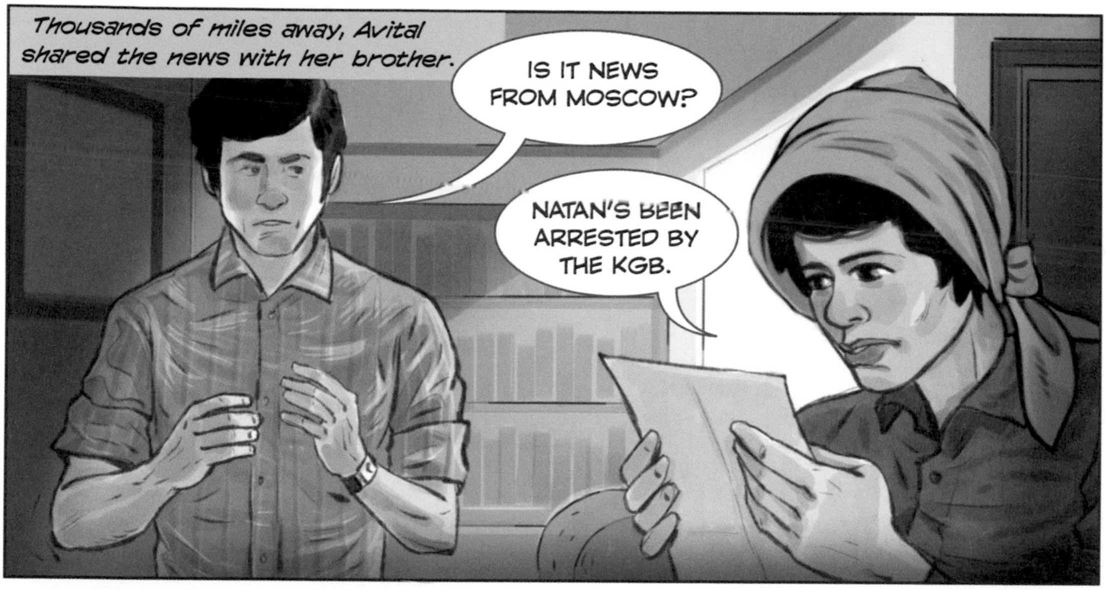
Thousands of miles away, Avital shared the news with her brother.
IS IT NEWS FROM MOSCOW?
NATAN'S BEEN ARRESTED BY THE KGB.

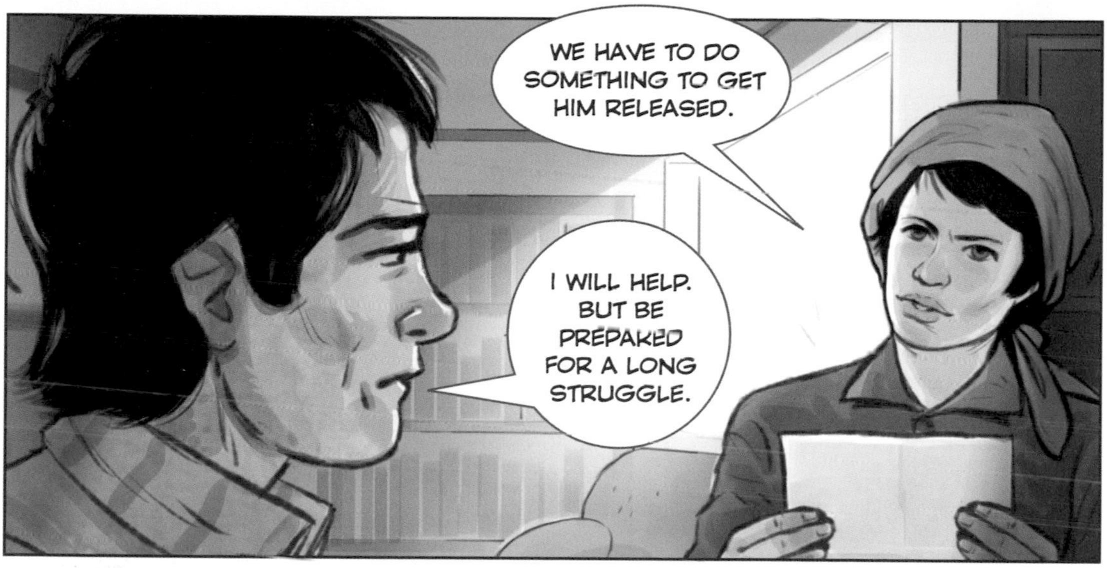
WE HAVE TO DO SOMETHING TO GET HIM RELEASED.
I WILL HELP. BUT BE PREPARED FOR A LONG STRUGGLE.

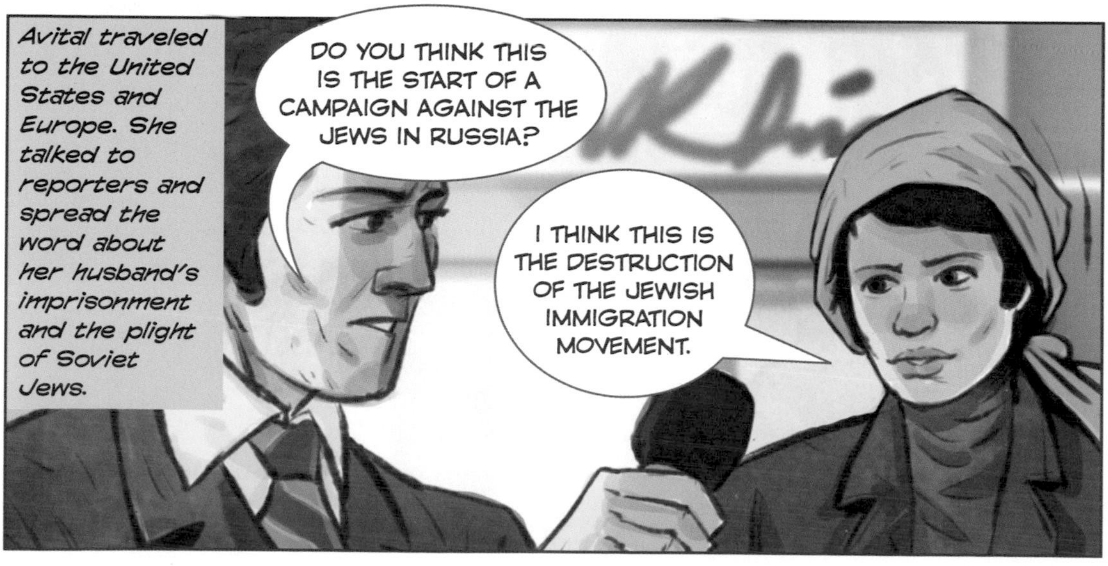
Avital traveled to the United States and Europe. She talked to reporters and spread the word about her husband's imprisonment and the plight of Soviet Jews.
DO YOU THINK THIS IS THE START OF A CAMPAIGN AGAINST THE JEWS IN RUSSIA?
I THINK THIS IS THE DESTRUCTION OF THE JEWISH IMMIGRATION MOVEMENT.

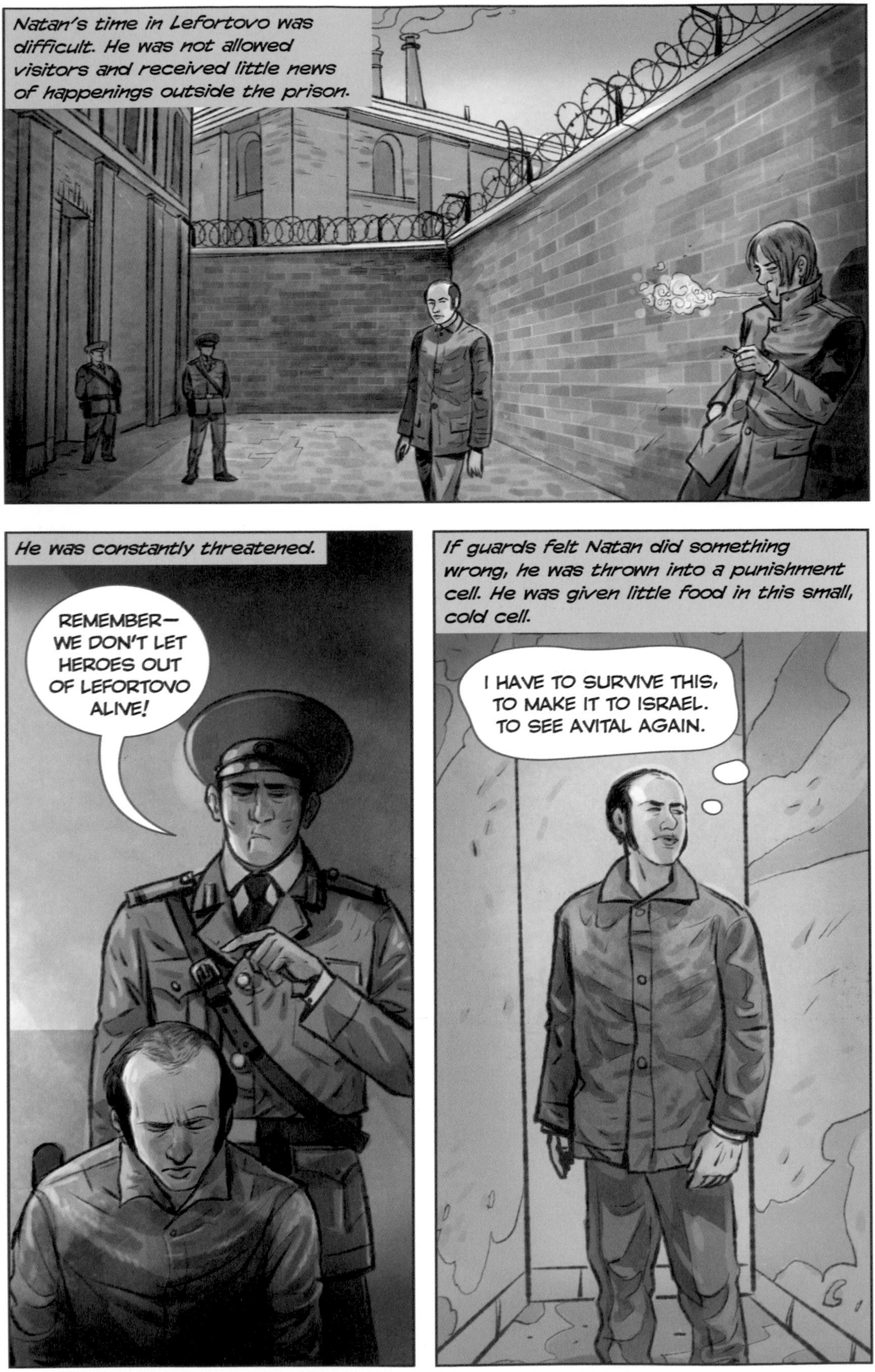
Natan's time in Lefortovo was difficult. He was not allowed visitors and received little news of happenings outside the prison.
He was constantly threatened.
REMEMBER— WE DON'T LET HEROES OUT OF LEFORTOVO ALIVE!
If guards felt Natan did something wrong, he was thrown into a punishment cell. He was given little food in this small, cold cell.
I HAVE TO SURVIVE THIS, TO MAKE IT TO ISRAEL. TO SEE AVITAL AGAIN.

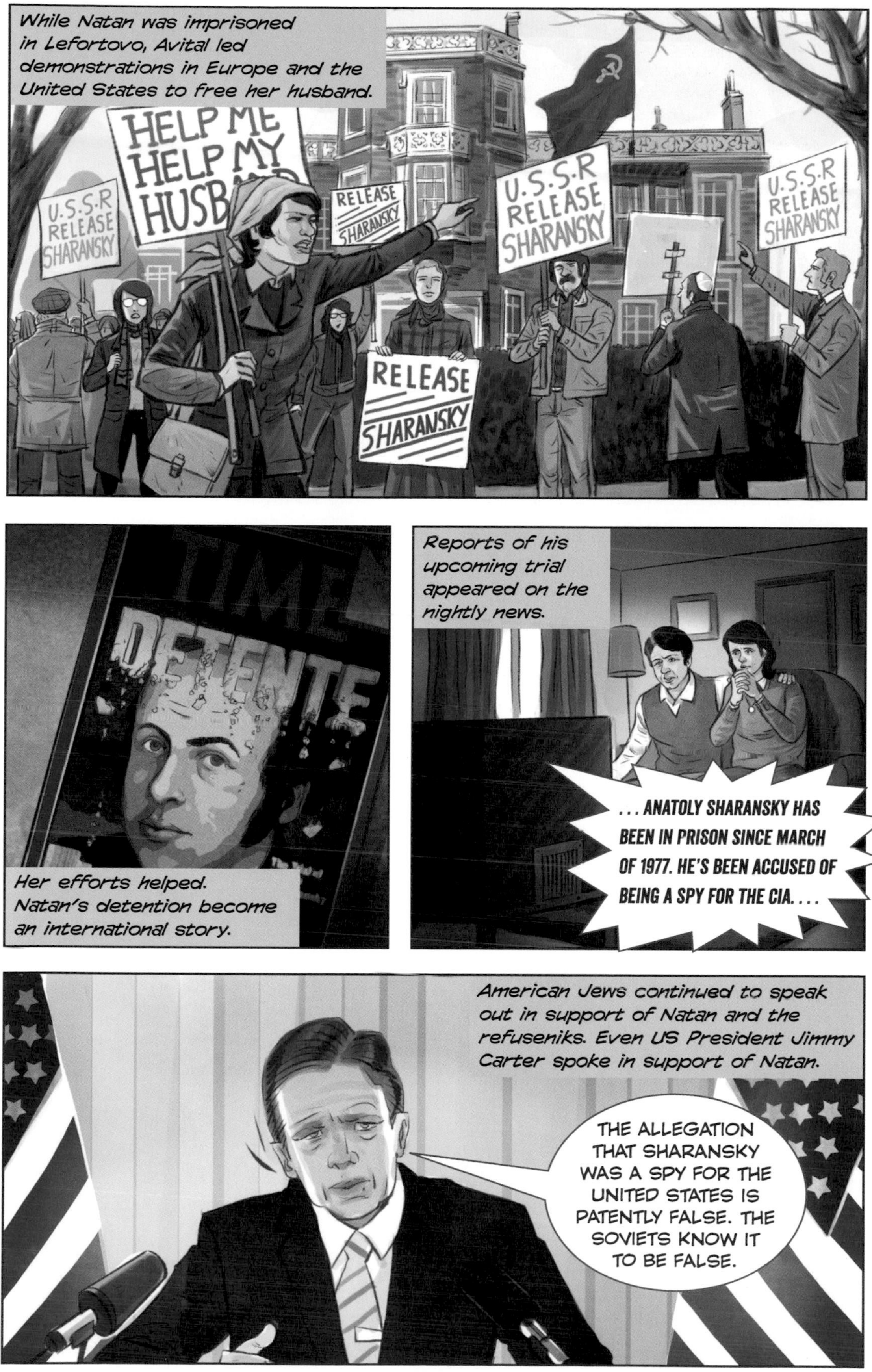
While Natan was imprisoned in Lefortovo, Avital led demonstrations in Europe and the United States to free her husband.
HELP ME HELP MY HUSB
U.S.S.R RELEASE SHARANSKY
RELEASE SHARANSKY
U.S.S.R RELEASE SHARANSKY
U.S.S.R RELEASE SHARANSKY
RELEASE SHARANSKY
TIME
DETENTE
Her efforts helped. Natan's detention become an international story.
Reports of his upcoming trial appeared on the nightly news.
. . . ANATOLY SHARANSKY HAS BEEN IN PRISON SINCE MARCH OF 1977. HE'S BEEN ACCUSED OF BEING A SPY FOR THE CIA. . . .
American Jews continued to speak out in support of Natan and the refuseniks. Even US President Jimmy Carter spoke in support of Natan.
THE ALLEGATION THAT SHARANSKY WAS A SPY FOR THE UNITED STATES IS PATENTLY FALSE. THE SOVIETS KNOW IT TO BE FALSE.

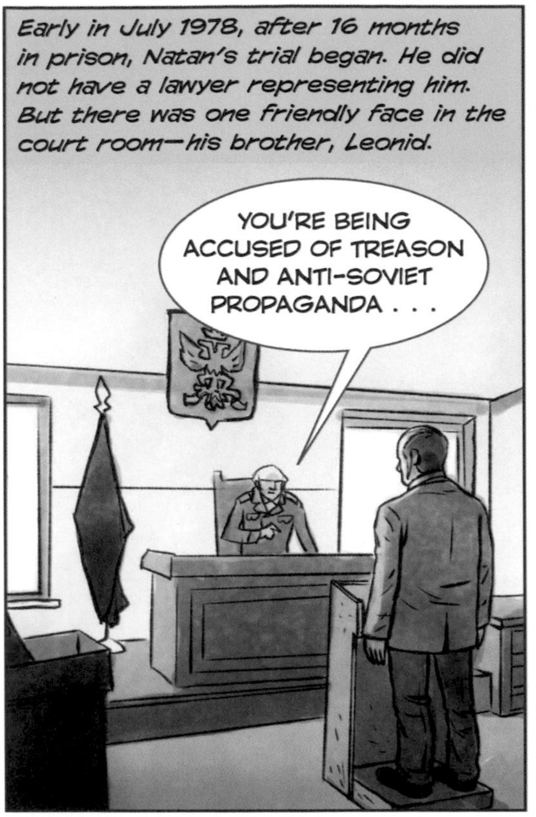
Early in July 1978, after 16 months in prison, Natan's trial began. He did not have a lawyer representing him. But there was one friendly face in the court room—his brother, Leonid.
YOU'RE BEING ACCUSED OF TREASON AND ANTI-SOVIET PROPAGANDA . . .

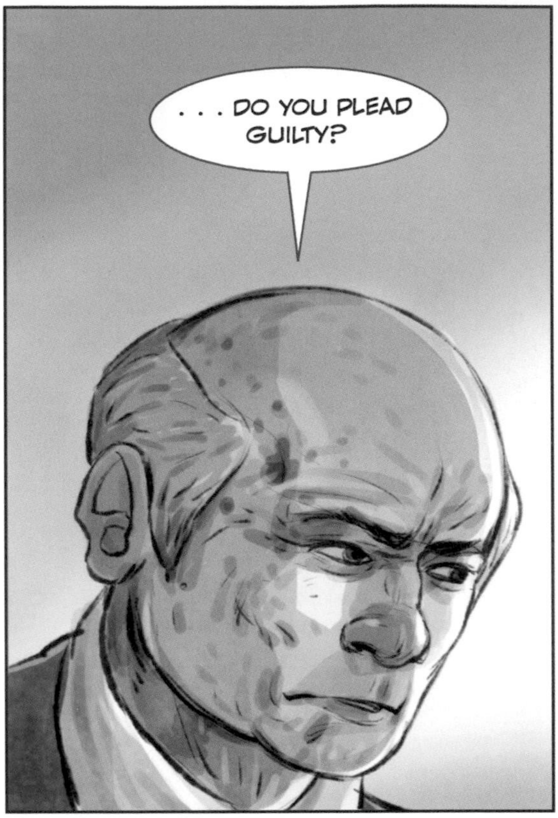
. . . DO YOU PLEAD GUILTY?

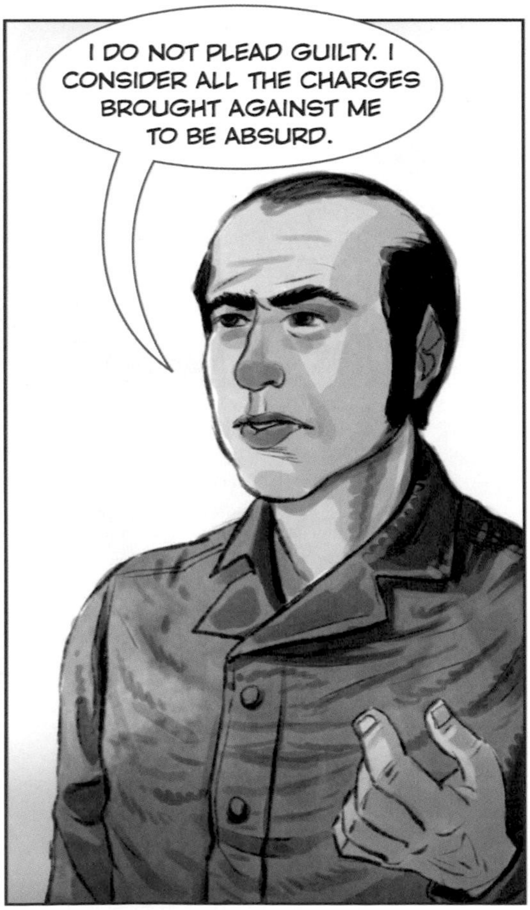
I DO NOT PLEAD GUILTY. I CONSIDER ALL THE CHARGES BROUGHT AGAINST ME TO BE ABSURD.

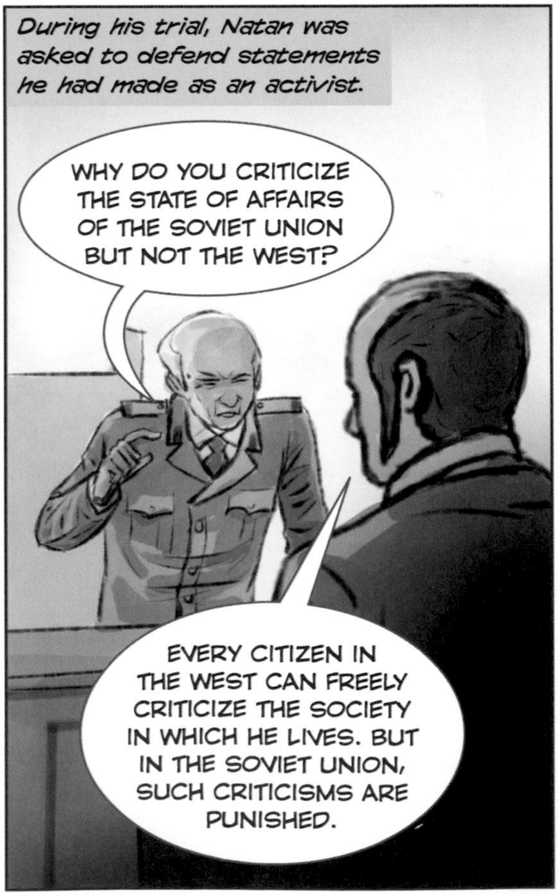
During his trial, Natan was asked to defend statements he had made as an activist.
WHY DO YOU CRITICIZE THE STATE OF AFFAIRS OF THE SOVIET UNION BUT NOT THE WEST?
EVERY CITIZEN IN THE WEST CAN FREELY CRITICIZE THE SOCIETY IN WHICH HE LIVES. BUT IN THE SOVIET UNION, SUCH CRITICISMS ARE PUNISHED.

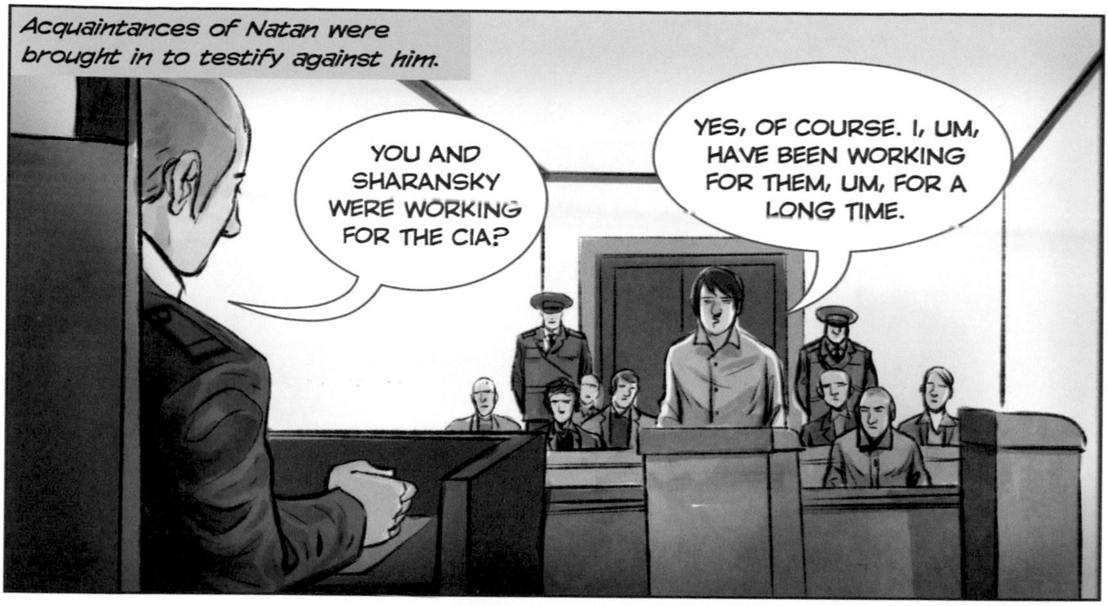
Acquaintances of Natan were brought in to testify against him.
YOU AND SHARANSKY WERE WORKING FOR THE CIA?
YES, OF COURSE. I, UM, HAVE BEEN WORKING FOR THEM, UM, FOR A LONG TIME.

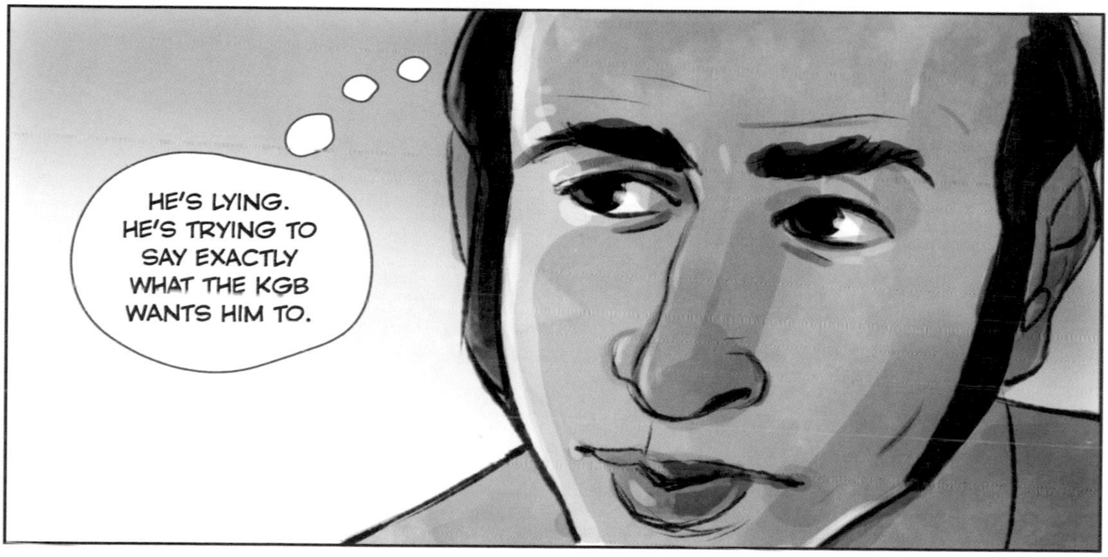
HE'S LYING. HE'S TRYING TO SAY EXACTLY WHAT THE KGB WANTS HIM TO.

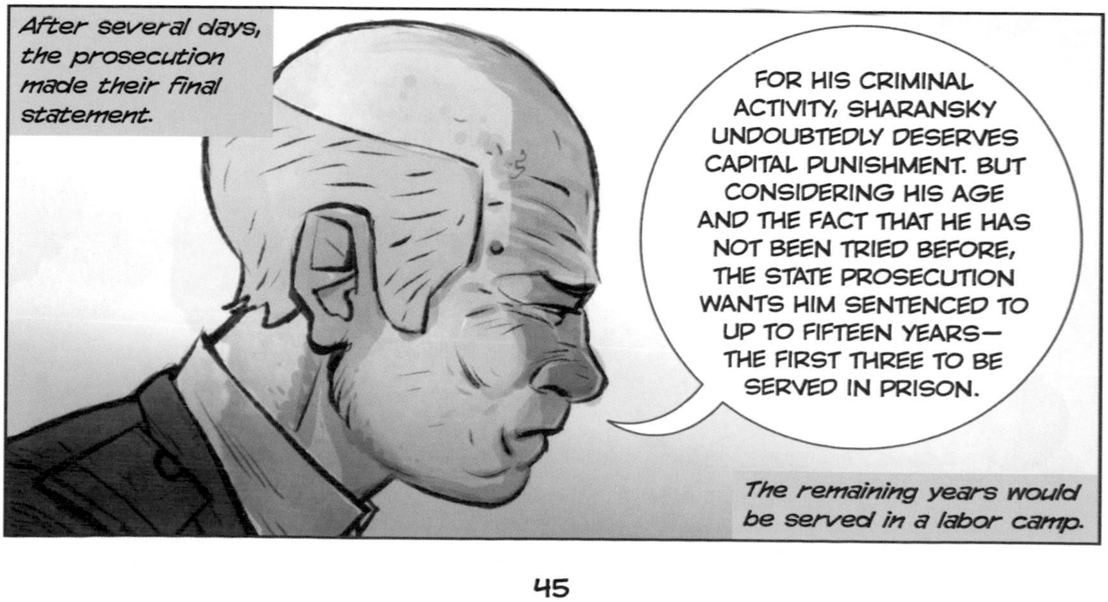
After several days, the prosecution made their final statement.
FOR HIS CRIMINAL ACTIVITY, SHARANSKY UNDOUBTEDLY DESERVES CAPITAL PUNISHMENT. BUT CONSIDERING HIS AGE AND THE FACT THAT HE HAS NOT BEEN TRIED BEFORE, THE STATE PROSECUTION WANTS HIM SENTENCED TO UP TO FIFTEEN YEARS— THE FIRST THREE TO BE SERVED IN PRISON.
The remaining years would be served in a labor camp.

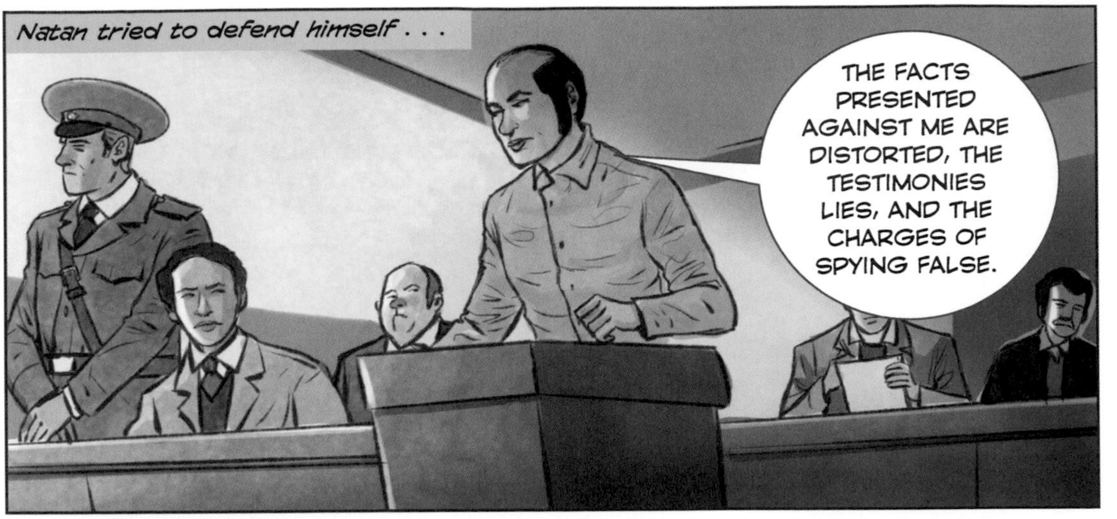
Natan tried to defend himself . . .
THE FACTS PRESENTED AGAINST ME ARE DISTORTED, THE TESTIMONIES LIES, AND THE CHARGES OF SPYING FALSE.

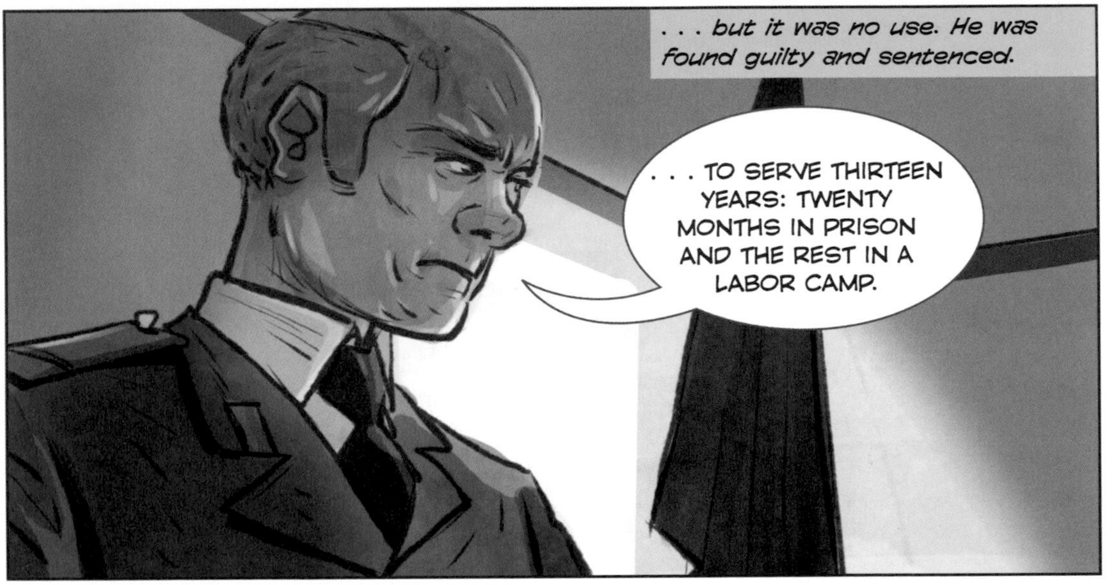
. . . but it was no use. He was found guilty and sentenced.
. . . TO SERVE THIRTEEN YEARS: TWENTY MONTHS IN PRISON AND THE REST IN A LABOR CAMP.

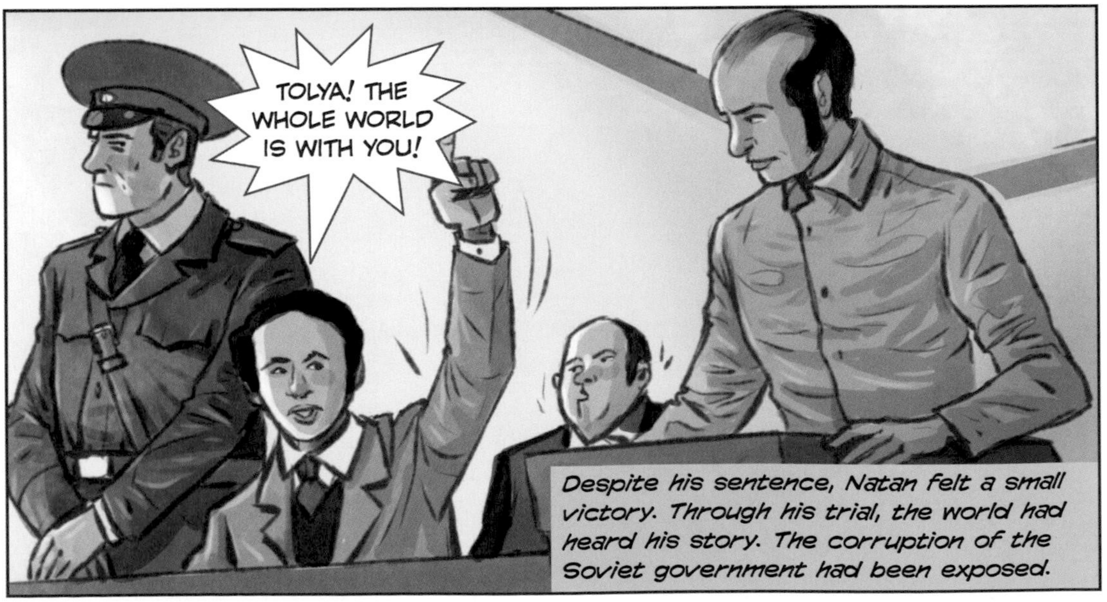
TOLYA! THE WHOLE WORLD IS WITH YOU!
Despite his sentence, Natan felt a small victory. Through his trial, the world had heard his story. The corruption of the Soviet government had been exposed.

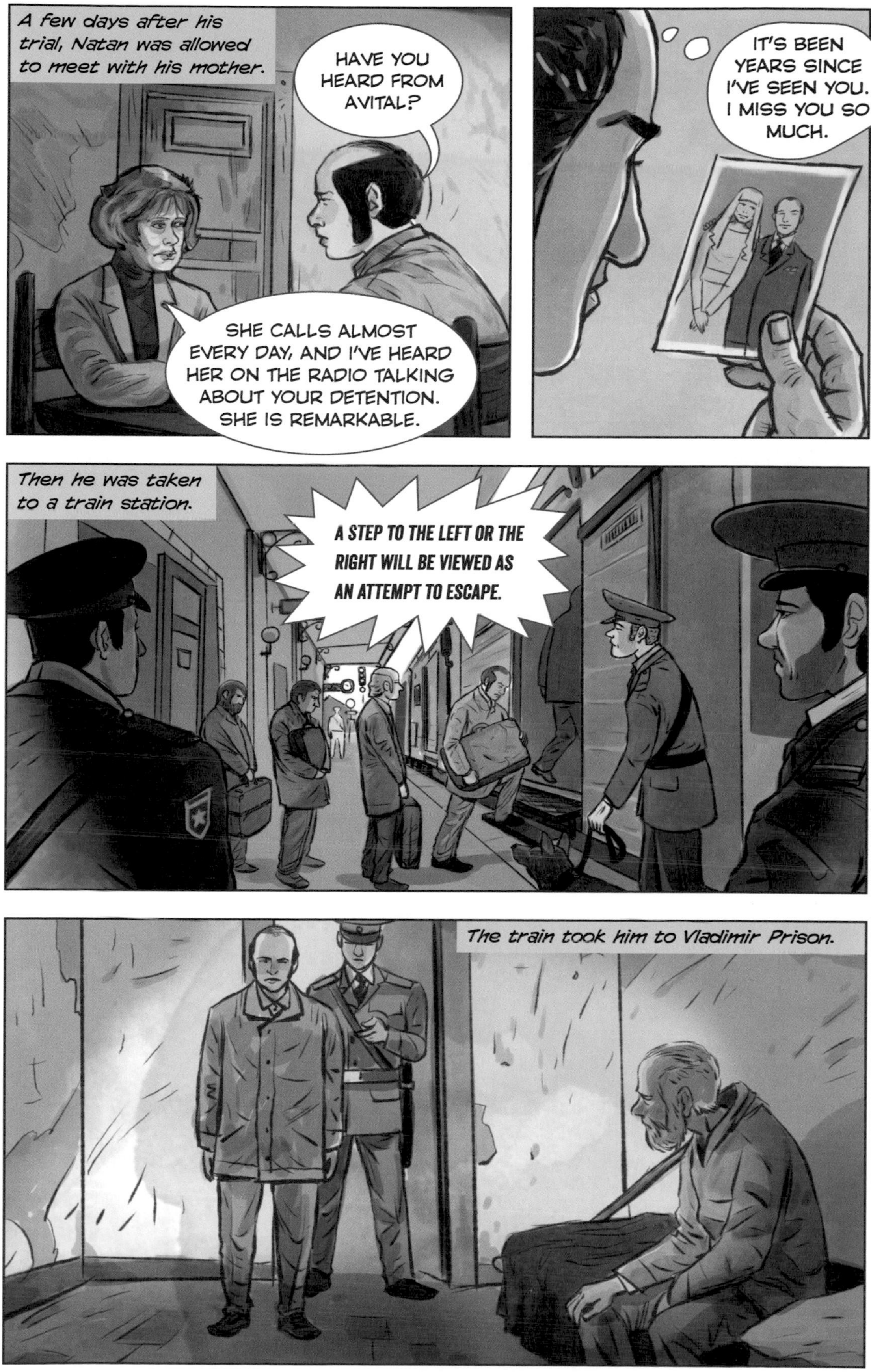
A few days after his trial, Natan was allowed to meet with his mother.
HAVE YOU HEARD FROM AVITAL?
SHE CALLS ALMOST EVERY DAY, AND I'VE HEARD HER ON THE RADIO TALKING ABOUT YOUR DETENTION. SHE IS REMARKABLE.
IT'S BEEN YEARS SINCE I'VE SEEN YOU. I MISS YOU SO MUCH.
Then he was taken to a train station.
A STEP TO THE LEFT OR THE RIGHT WILL BE VIEWED AS AN ATTEMPT TO ESCAPE.
The train took him to Vladimir Prison.

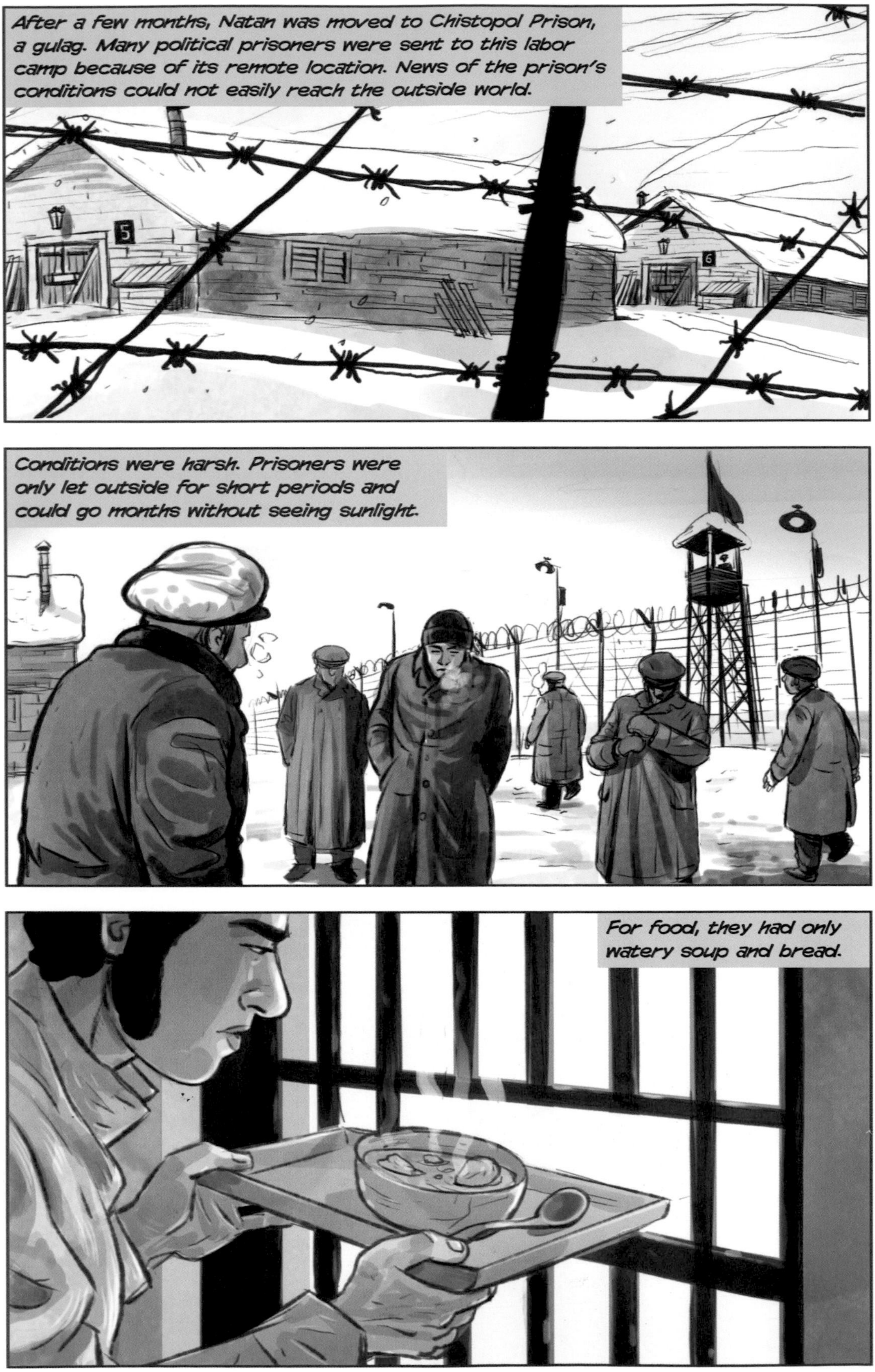
After a few months, Natan was moved to Chistopol Prison, a gulag. Many political prisoners were sent to this labor camp because of its remote location. News of the prison's conditions could not easily reach the outside world.
5
6
Conditions were harsh. Prisoners were only let outside for short periods and could go months without seeing sunlight.
For food, they had only watery soup and bread.

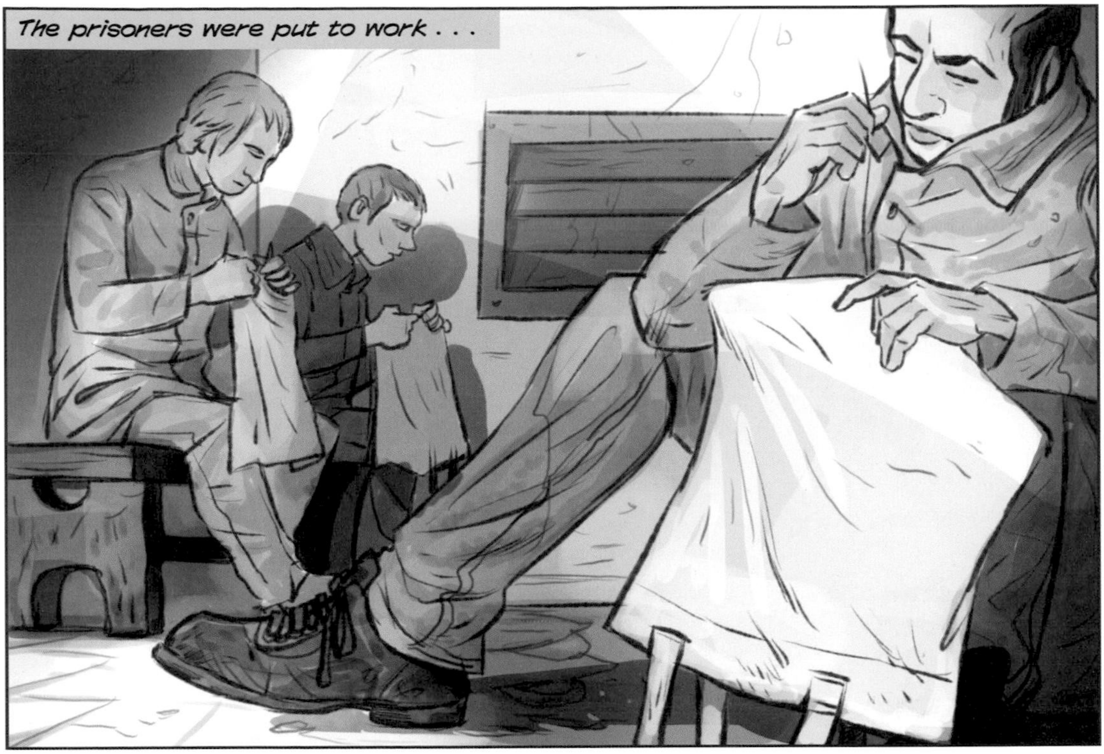
The prisoners were put to work . . .

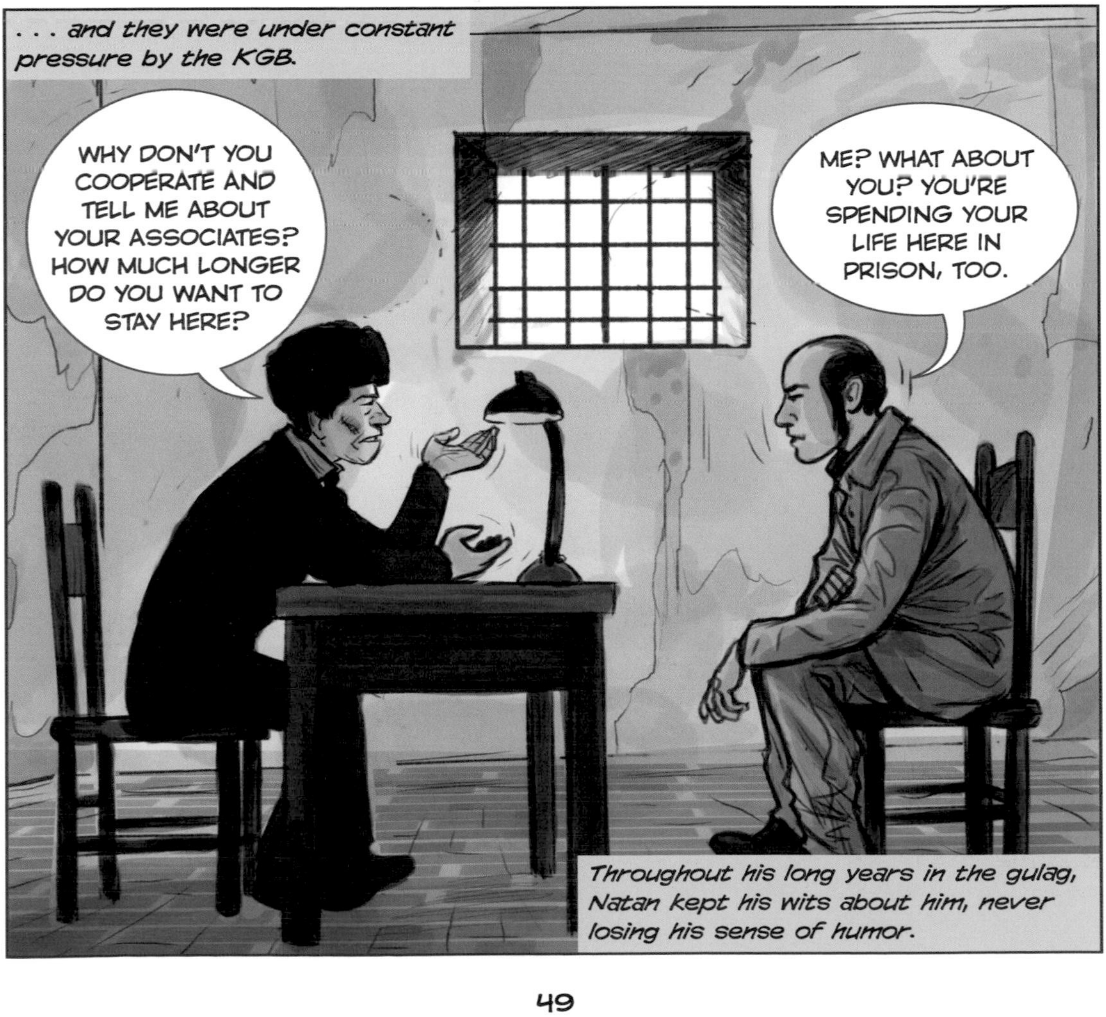
. . . and they were under constant pressure by the KGB.
WHY DON'T YOU COOPERATE AND TELL ME ABOUT YOUR ASSOCIATES? HOW MUCH LONGER DO YOU WANT TO STAY HERE?
ME? WHAT ABOUT YOU? YOU'RE SPENDING YOUR LIFE HERE IN PRISON, TOO.
Throughout his long years in the gulag, Natan kept his wits about him, never losing his sense of humor.

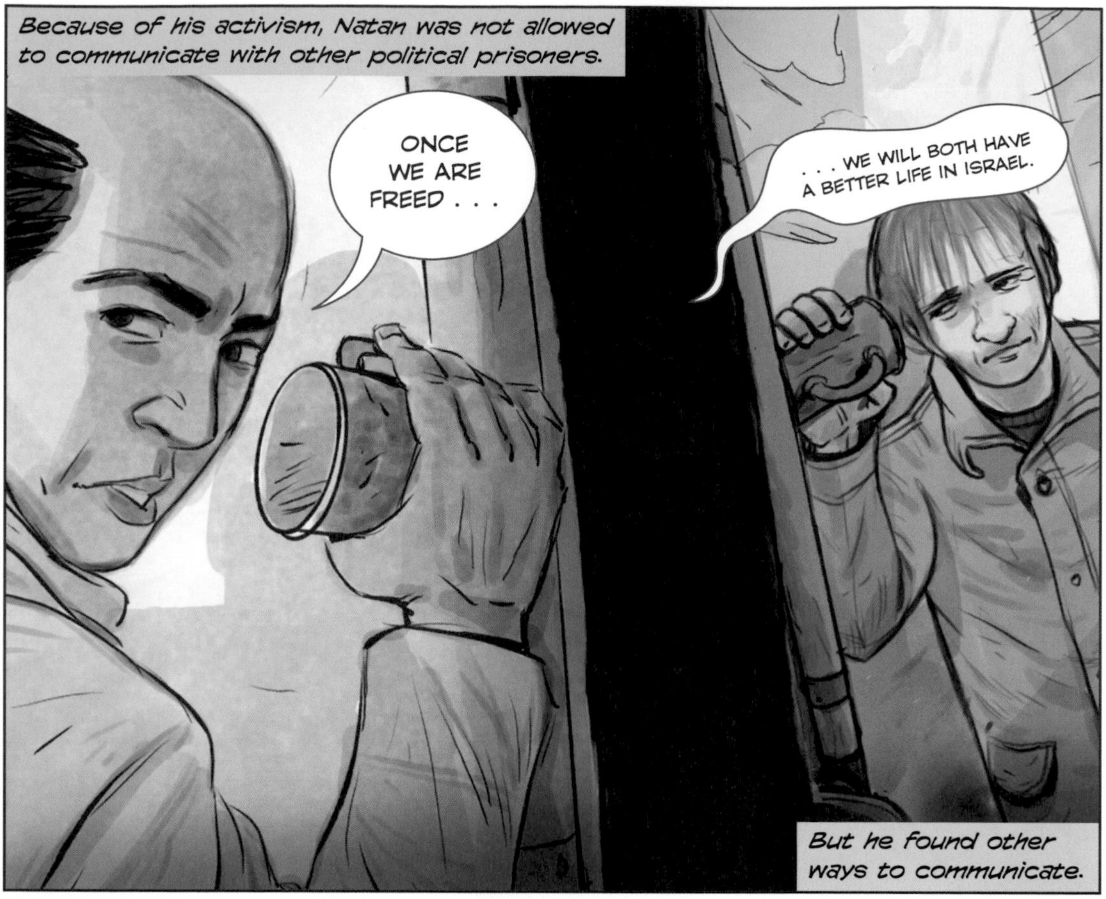
Because of his activism, Natan was not allowed to communicate with other political prisoners.
ONCE WE ARE FREED . . .
. . . WE WILL BOTH HAVE A BETTER LIFE IN ISRAEL.
But he found other ways to communicate.

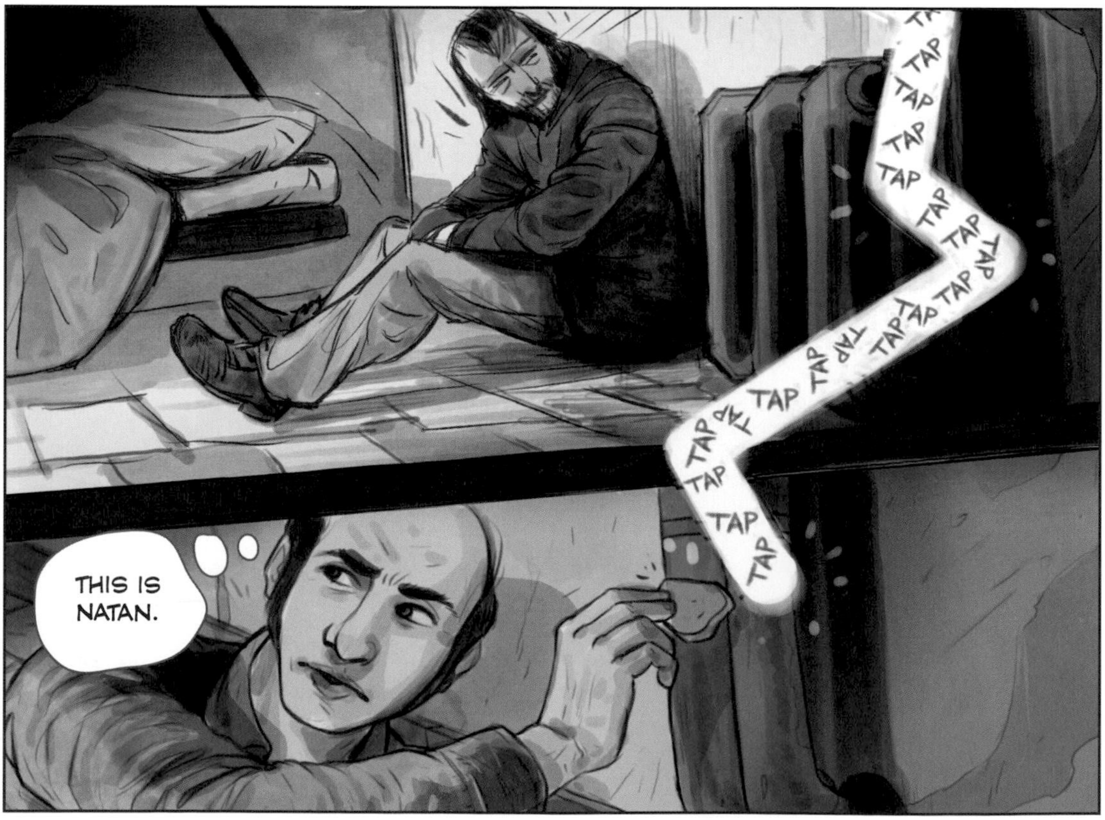
TAP TAP TAP TAP TAP TAP TAP TAP TAP TAP TAP TAP TAP TAP TAP TAP TAP TAP
THIS IS NATAN.

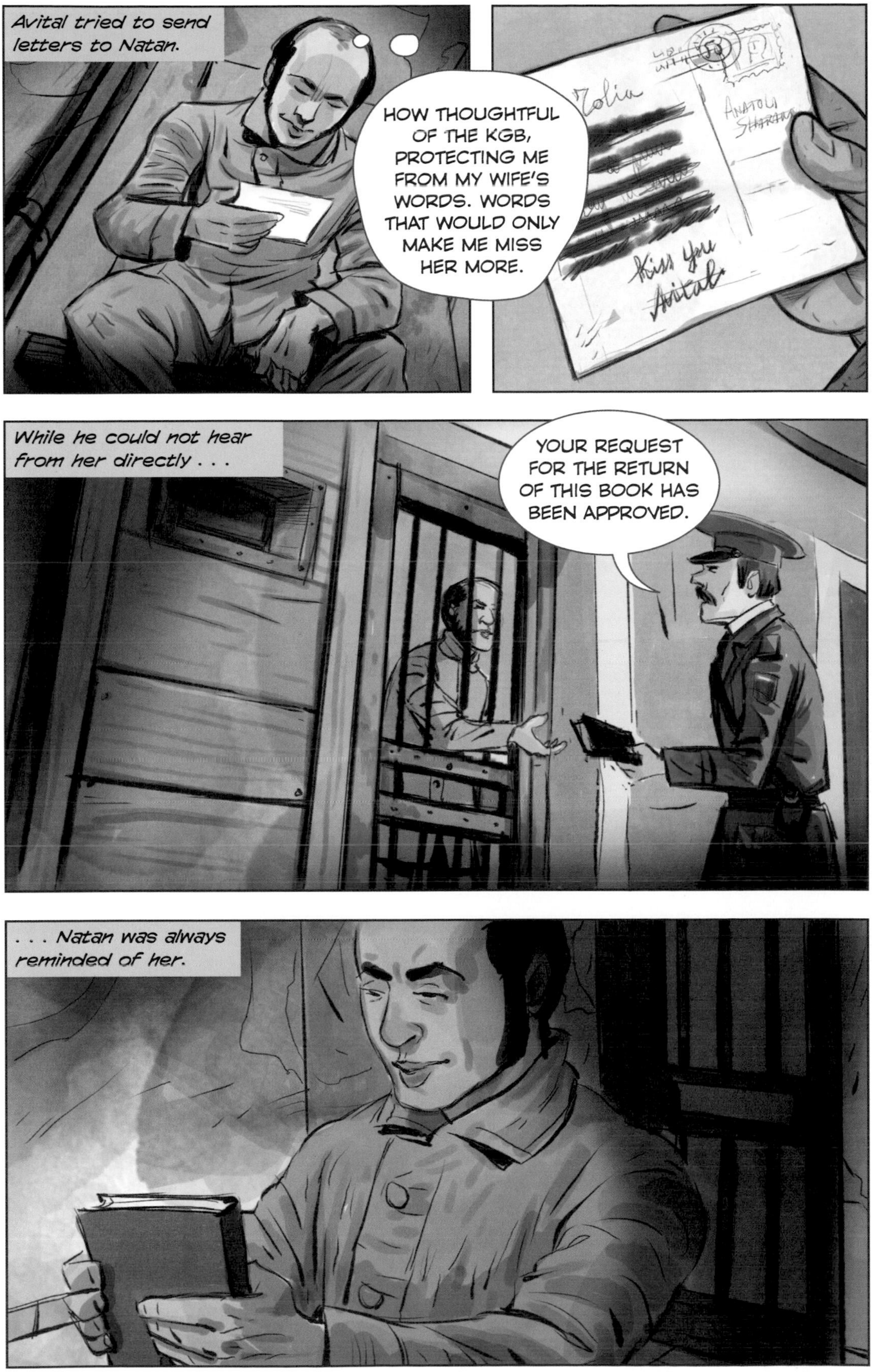
Avital tried to send letters to Natan.
HOW THOUGHTFUL OF THE KGB, PROTECTING ME FROM MY WIFE'S WORDS. WORDS THAT WOULD ONLY MAKE ME MISS HER MORE.
While he could not hear from her directly . . .
YOUR REQUEST FOR THE RETURN OF THIS BOOK HAS BEEN APPROVED.
. . . Natan was always reminded of her.

When Natan was caught doing something the guards did not like, such as trying to pass a message to another prisoner, he was sent to a punishment cell. He played chess in his head to keep his brain sharp.

Punishment cells were both physically and mentally taxing.

I THINK HE'S LOSING HIS MIND.

SHH, I'M THINKING OF MY NEXT MOVE.

In total, Natan would spend more than 400 days in punishment cells.

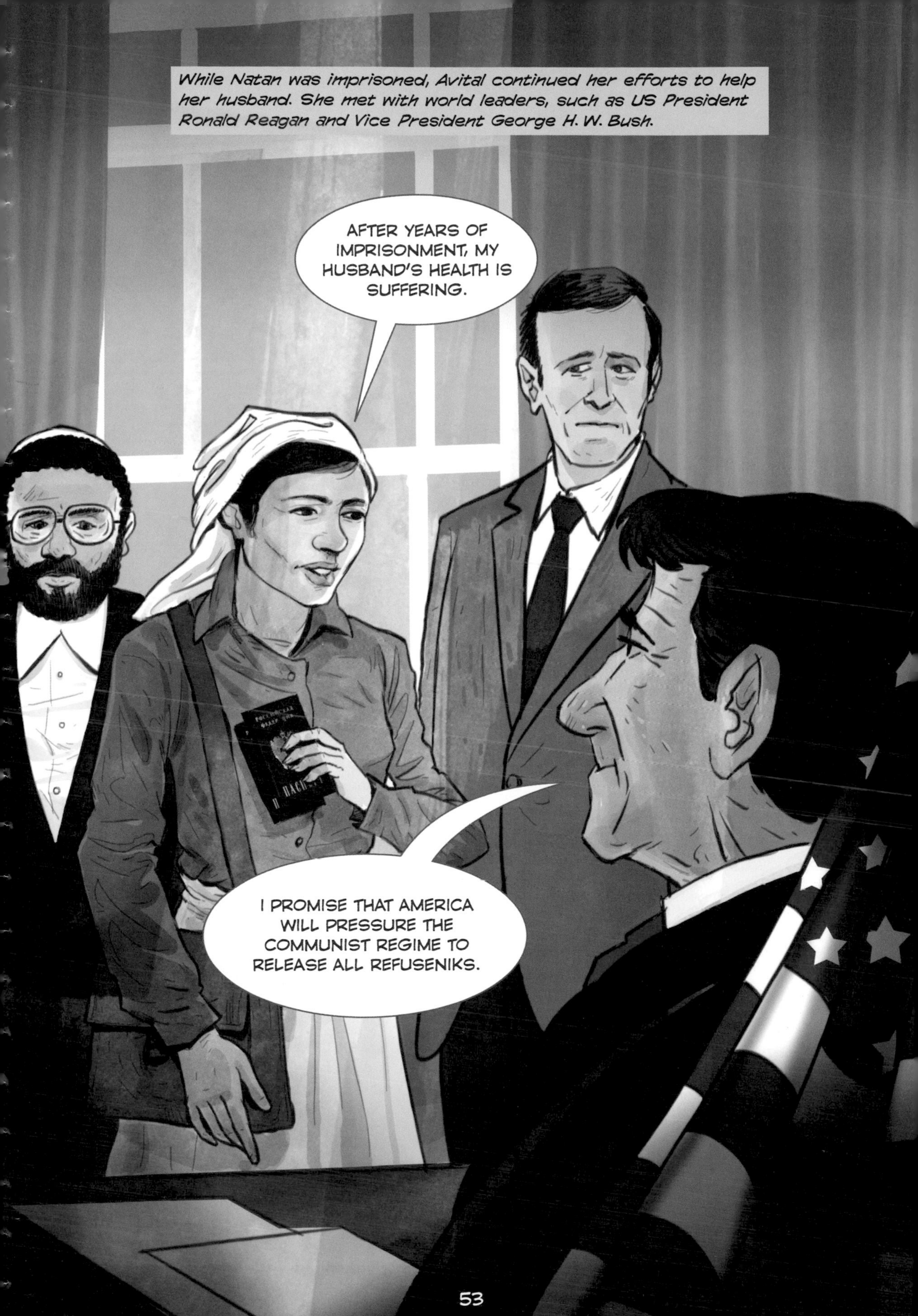
While Natan was imprisoned, Avital continued her efforts to help her husband. She met with world leaders, such as US President Ronald Reagan and Vice President George H. W. Bush.
AFTER YEARS OF IMPRISONMENT, MY HUSBAND'S HEALTH IS SUFFERING.
I PROMISE THAT AMERICA WILL PRESSURE THE COMMUNIST REGIME TO RELEASE ALL REFUSENIKS.

5 ALIYAH

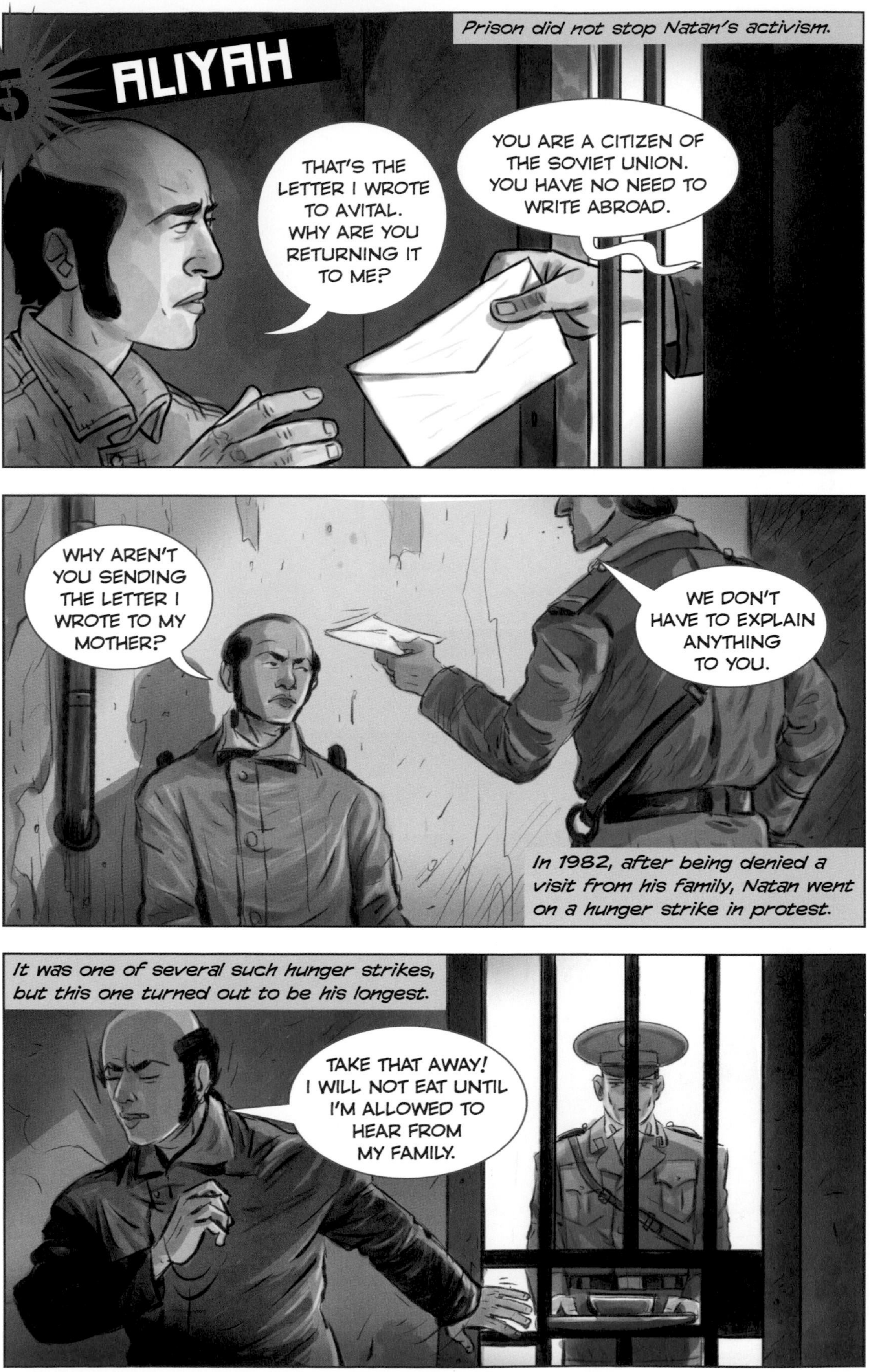

Prison did not stop Natan's activism.
THAT'S THE LETTER I WROTE TO AVITAL. WHY ARE YOU RETURNING IT TO ME?
YOU ARE A CITIZEN OF THE SOVIET UNION. YOU HAVE NO NEED TO WRITE ABROAD.
WHY AREN'T YOU SENDING THE LETTER I WROTE TO MY MOTHER?
WE DON'T HAVE TO EXPLAIN ANYTHING TO YOU.
In 1982, after being denied a visit from his family, Natan went on a hunger strike in protest.
It was one of several such hunger strikes, but this one turned out to be his longest.
TAKE THAT AWAY! I WILL NOT EAT UNTIL I'M ALLOWED TO HEAR FROM MY FAMILY.

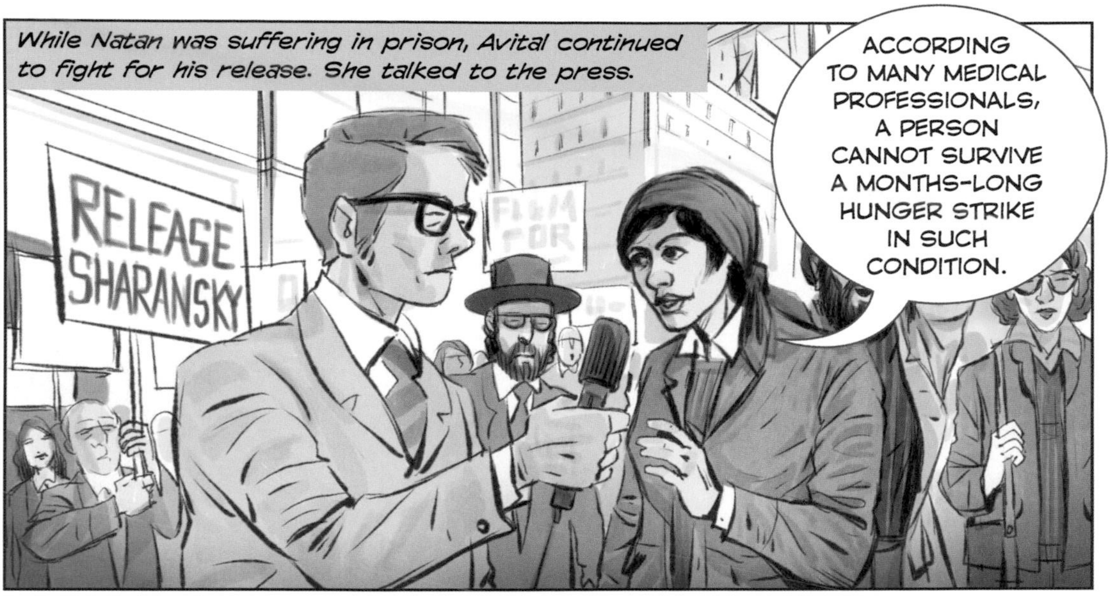
While Natan was suffering in prison, Avital continued to fight for his release. She talked to the press.
RELEASE SHARANSKY
ACCORDING TO MANY MEDICAL PROFESSIONALS, A PERSON CANNOT SURVIVE A MONTHS-LONG HUNGER STRIKE IN SUCH CONDITION.

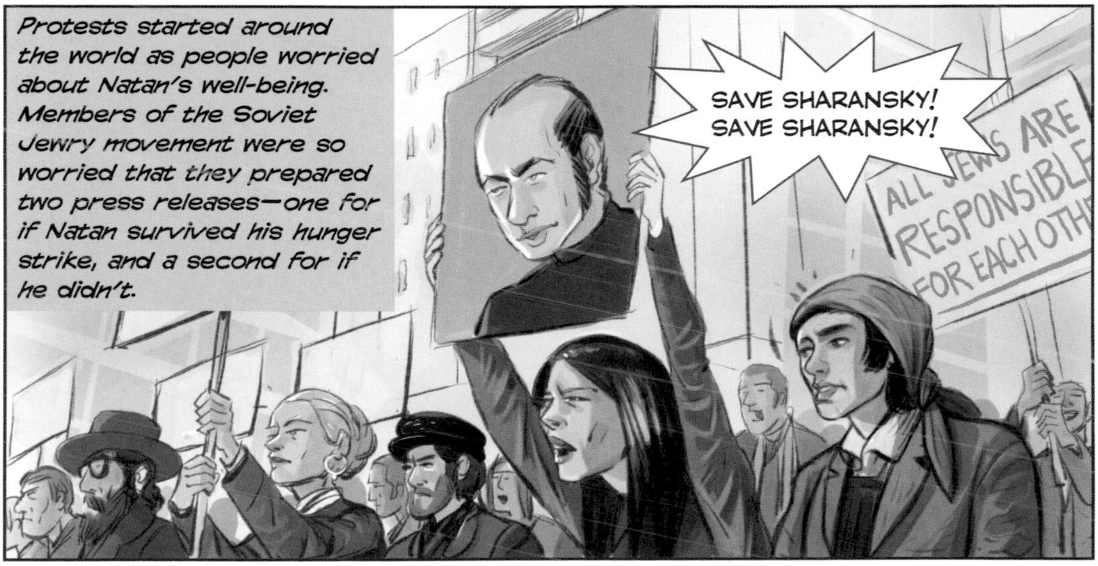
Protests started around the world as people worried about Natan's well-being. Members of the Soviet Jewry movement were so worried that they prepared two press releases—one for if Natan survived his hunger strike, and a second for if he didn't.
SAVE SHARANSKY! SAVE SHARANSKY!

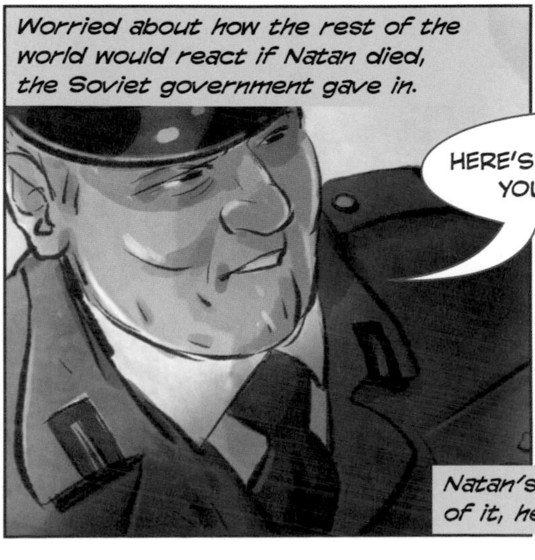
Worried about how the rest of the world would react if Natan died, the Soviet government gave in.
HERE'S A LETTER FROM YOUR MOTHER.

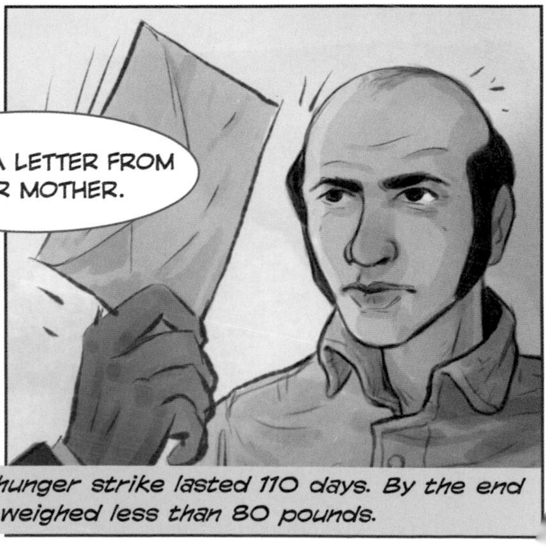
Natan's hunger strike lasted 110 days. By the end of it, he weighed less than 80 pounds.

Shortly after Natan's hunger strike ended, Avital received a letter from President Reagan.

I am writing to confirm my continuing concern and support for your husband Anatoly . . . I remain willing to pursue every possible avenue to improve his situation and secure his freedom.

In 1985, Konstantin Chernenko, the leader of the Soviet Union, died. Mikhail Gorbachev became General Secretary of the communist party.

As Gorbachev traveled to meet other world leaders, he was met by protestors wherever he went, starting in France.

LIBEREZ ANATOLY

FREE SOVIET JEWS!

LIBEREZ ANATOLY

LIBEREZ

LIBEREZ ANATOLY

LIBEREZ ANATOLY

LIB ANATOLY

ANAT

FREE SOVIET JEWS!

LIBEREZ ANATOLY

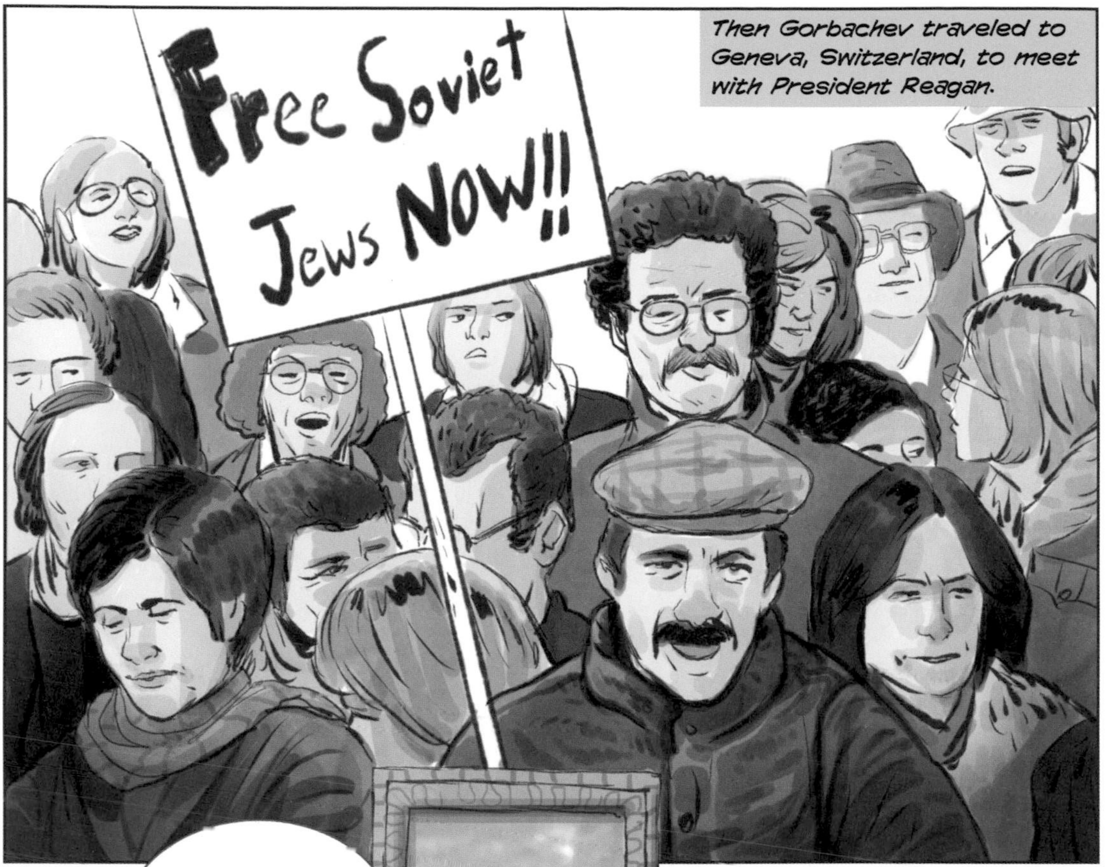
Then Gorbachev traveled to Geneva, Switzerland, to meet with President Reagan.
Free Soviet Jews NOW!!

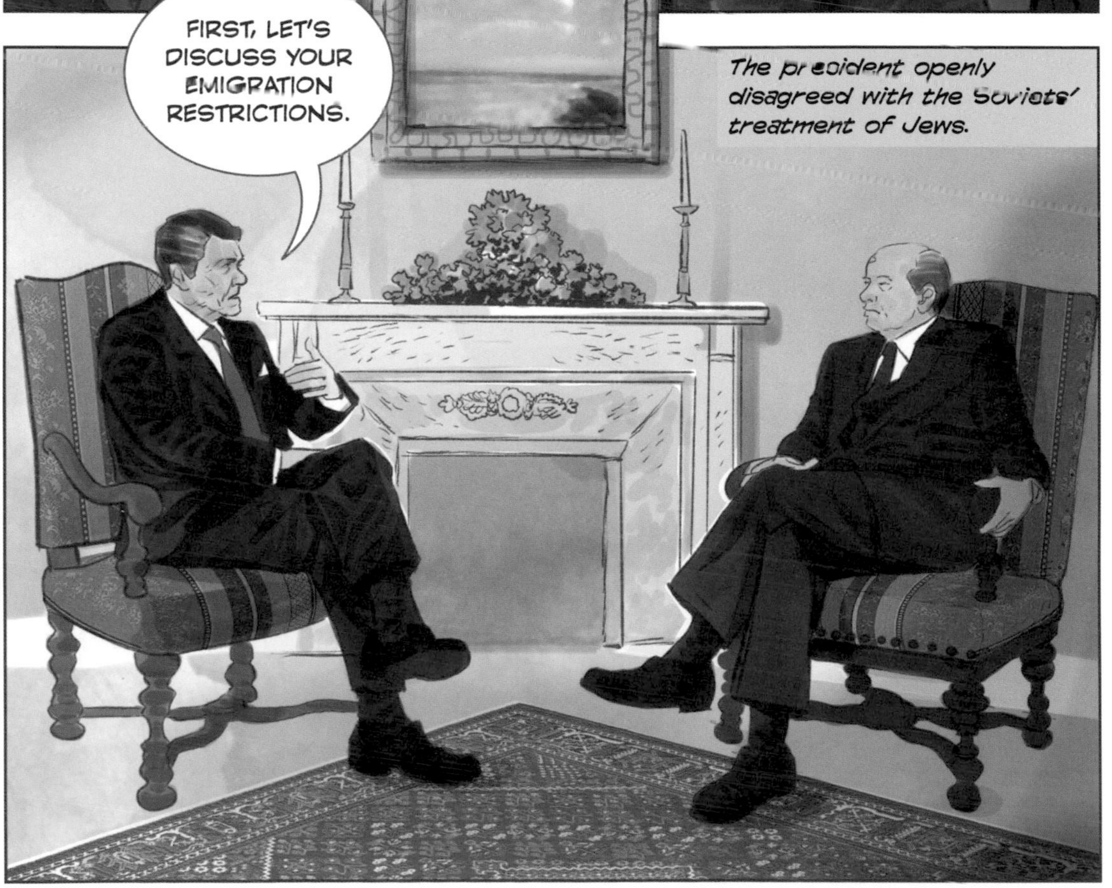
FIRST, LET'S DISCUSS YOUR EMIGRATION RESTRICTIONS.
The president openly disagreed with the Soviets' treatment of Jews.

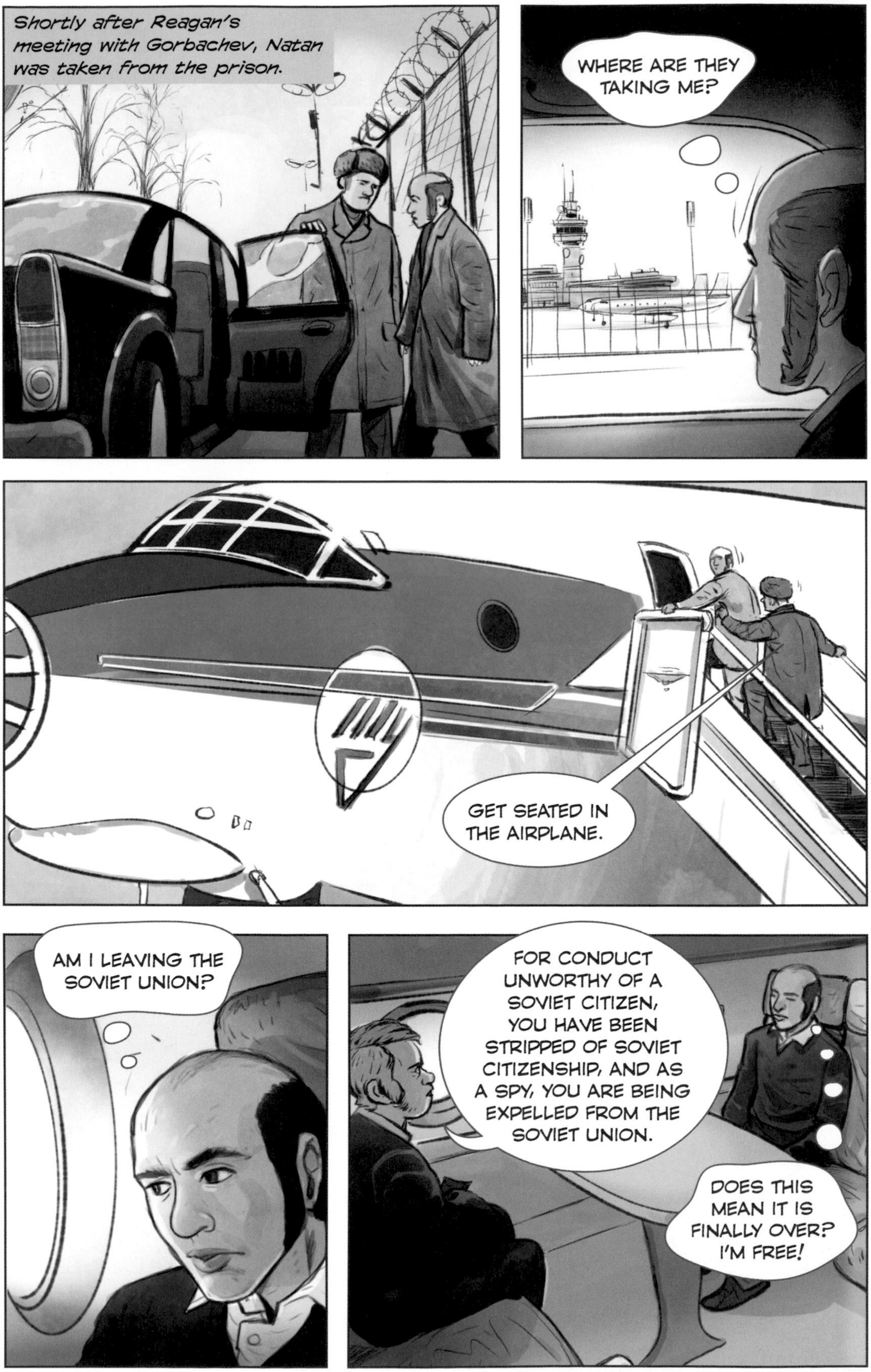
Shortly after Reagan's meeting with Gorbachev, Natan was taken from the prison.
WHERE ARE THEY TAKING ME?
GET SEATED IN THE AIRPLANE.
AM I LEAVING THE SOVIET UNION?
FOR CONDUCT UNWORTHY OF A SOVIET CITIZEN, YOU HAVE BEEN STRIPPED OF SOVIET CITIZENSHIP, AND AS A SPY, YOU ARE BEING EXPELLED FROM THE SOVIET UNION.
DOES THIS MEAN IT IS FINALLY OVER? I'M FREE!

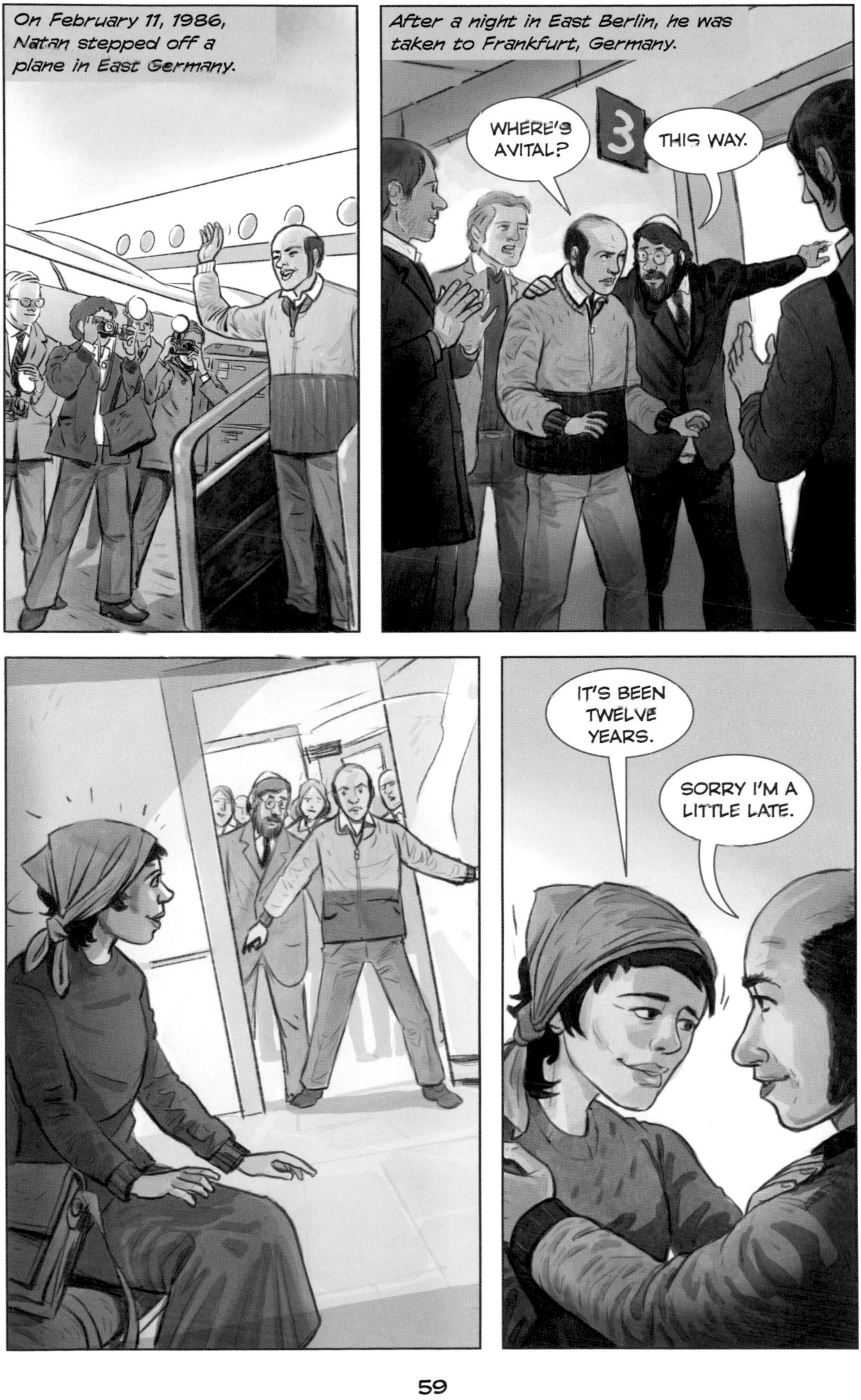
On February 11, 1986, Natan stepped off a plane in East Germany.
After a night in East Berlin, he was taken to Frankfurt, Germany.
WHERE'S AVITAL?
3
THIS WAY.
IT'S BEEN TWELVE YEARS.
SORRY I'M A LITTLE LATE.

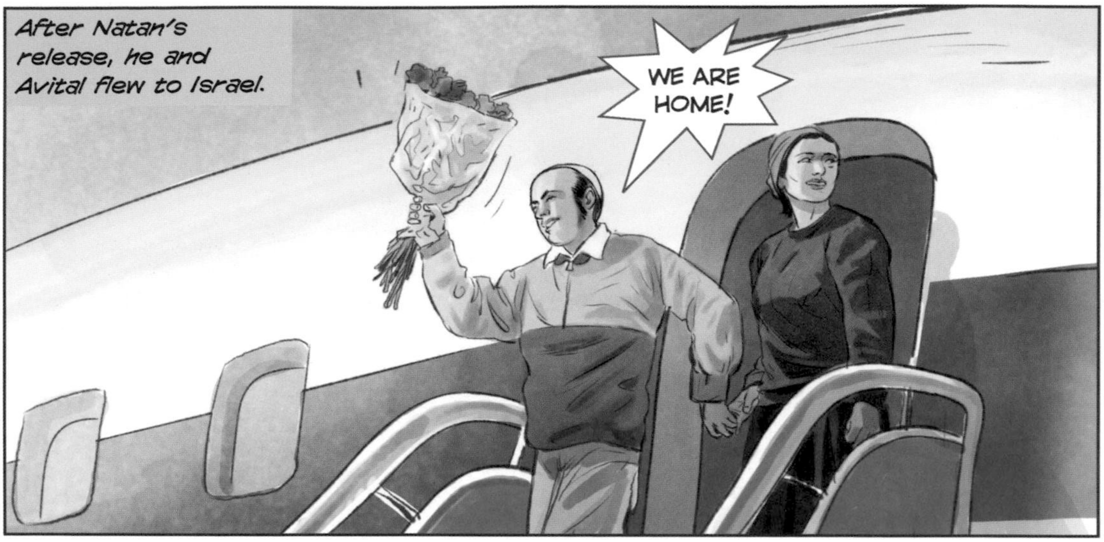
After Natan's release, he and Avital flew to Israel.
WE ARE HOME!

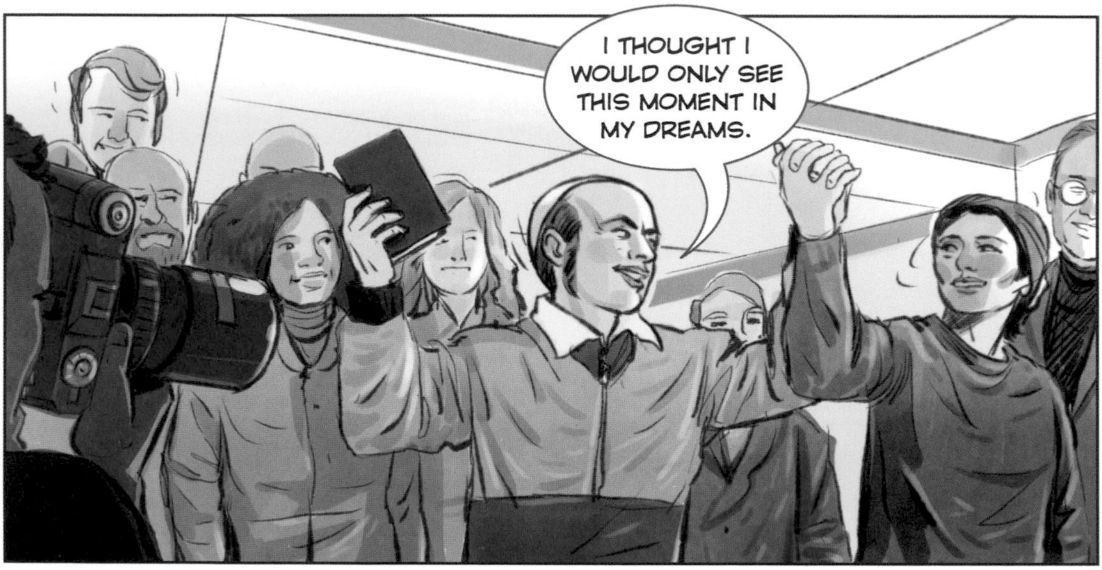
I THOUGHT I WOULD ONLY SEE THIS MOMENT IN MY DREAMS.

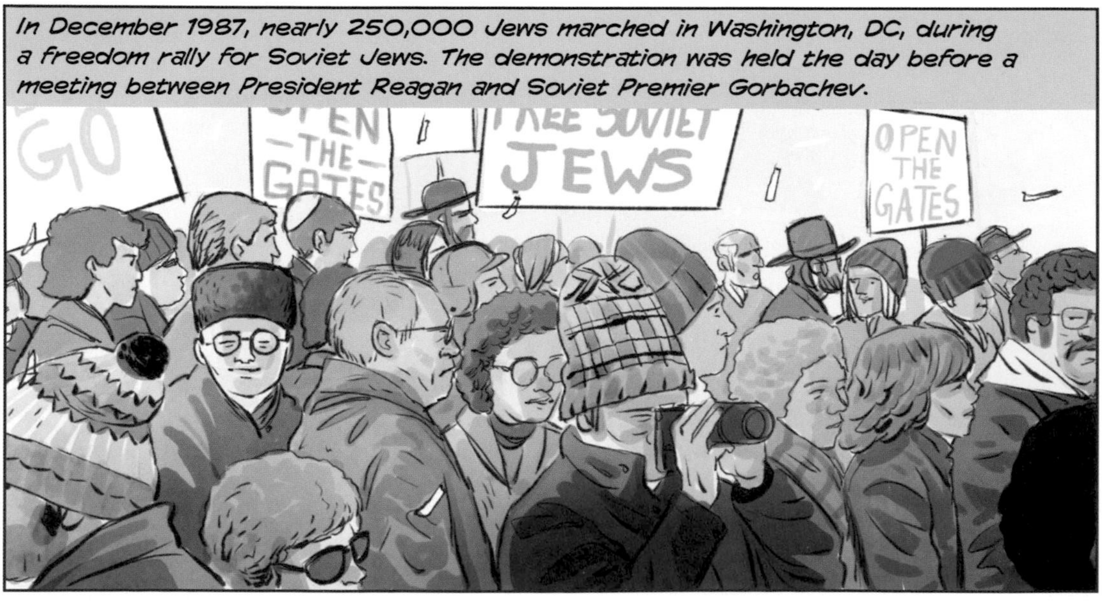
In December 1987, nearly 250,000 Jews marched in Washington, DC, during a freedom rally for Soviet Jews. The demonstration was held the day before a meeting between President Reagan and Soviet Premier Gorbachev.
FREE SOVIET JEWS
OPEN THE GATES

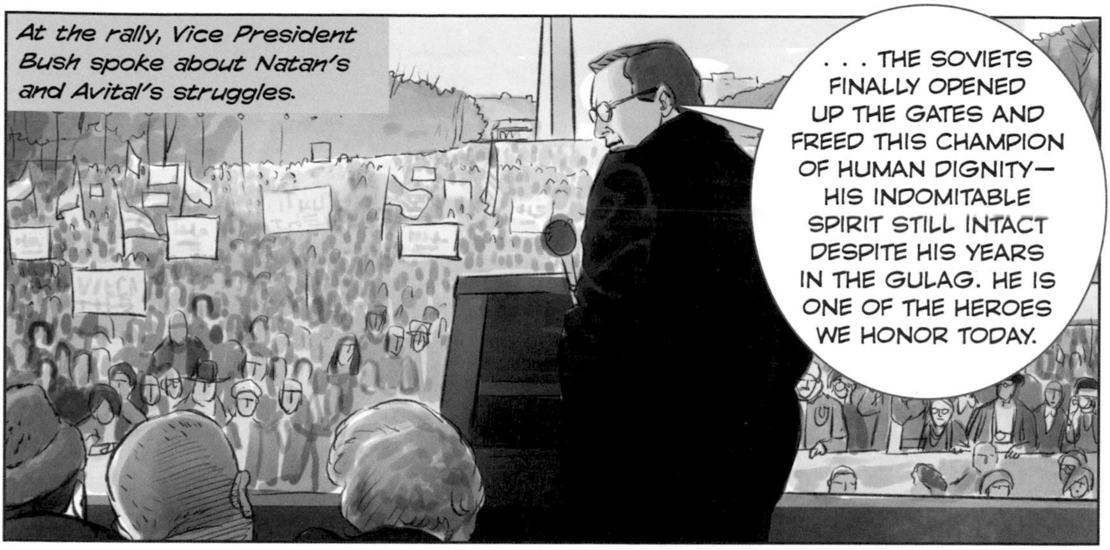
At the rally, Vice President Bush spoke about Natan's and Avital's struggles.
. . . THE SOVIETS FINALLY OPENED UP THE GATES AND FREED THIS CHAMPION OF HUMAN DIGNITY—HIS INDOMITABLE SPIRIT STILL INTACT DESPITE HIS YEARS IN THE GULAG. HE IS ONE OF THE HEROES WE HONOR TODAY.

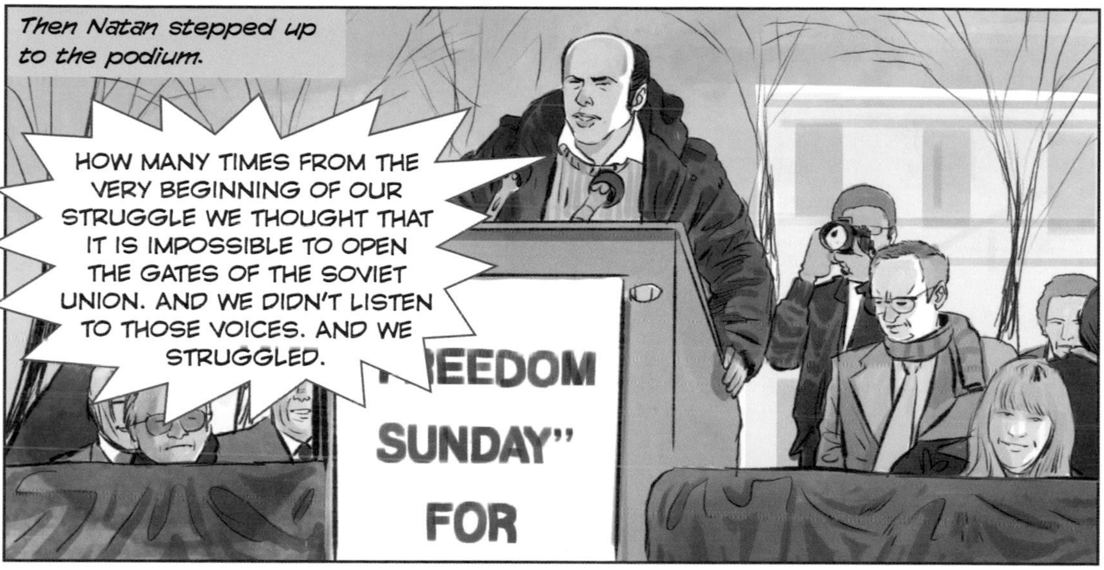
Then Natan stepped up to the podium.
HOW MANY TIMES FROM THE VERY BEGINNING OF OUR STRUGGLE WE THOUGHT THAT IT IS IMPOSSIBLE TO OPEN THE GATES OF THE SOVIET UNION. AND WE DIDN'T LISTEN TO THOSE VOICES. AND WE STRUGGLED.
REEDOM
SUNDAY"
FOR

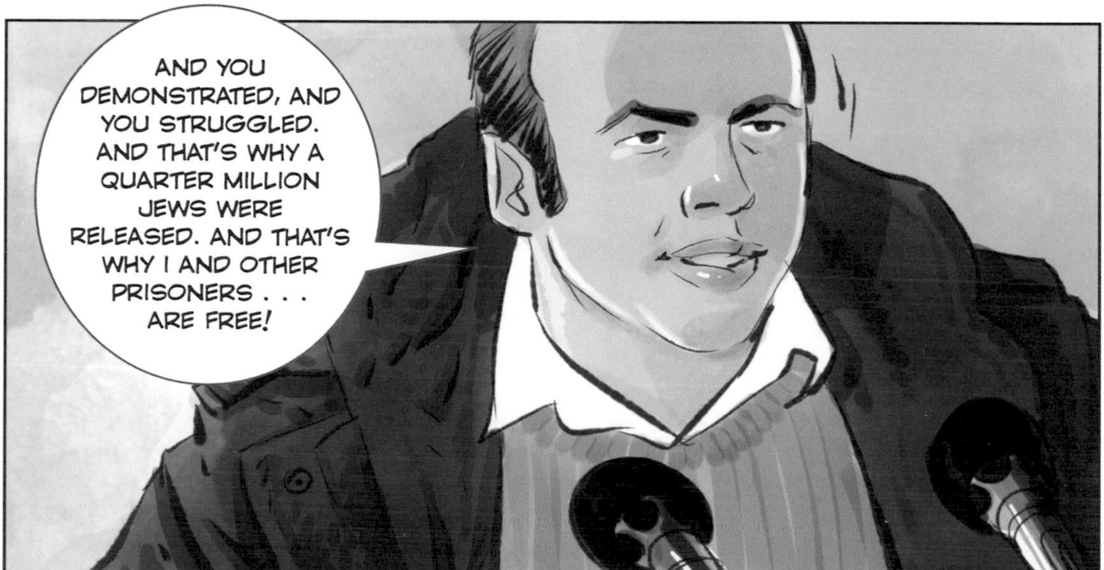
AND YOU DEMONSTRATED, AND YOU STRUGGLED. AND THAT'S WHY A QUARTER MILLION JEWS WERE RELEASED. AND THAT'S WHY I AND OTHER PRISONERS . . . ARE FREE!

AFTERWORD

Sharansky visits with American Soviet Jewry activists. *From right: Herbert Kohn, Sharansky, Harry Lerner, Stephen Feinstein*

Natan Sharansky in Israel

Israeli prime minister Benjamin Netanyahu watches as Sharansky *(right)* plays chess against Israeli Chess International Grandmaster Boris Gelfand.

After settling in Israel, Natan Sharansky continued to support Soviet Jews. He founded and became president of the Zionist Forum, a group that helps new immigrants find housing and jobs in Israel.

To help the many Jews who were emigrating from the Soviet Union to Israel, Sharansky became involved in politics. In 1996, he helped form the Israeli political party Yisrael b'Aliyah, which focused on aiding new arrivals from the Soviet Union. Due to the support his party received in that election, Sharansky was appointed as the government's minister of industry and trade.

During his time in politics, Sharansky held several posts, including Minister of the Interior and Deputy Prime Minster. He continues to work to help Jews living outside of Israel. He resigned from politics in 2006 and served as chairman of the Jewish Agency for Israel.

Sharansky and Avital have two daughters, Rachel and Hannah. Sharansky continues to be active in human rights work. He and Avital have both written books about their experiences and struggles during the Soviet Jewry movement. Sharansky also continues to be a masterful chess player.

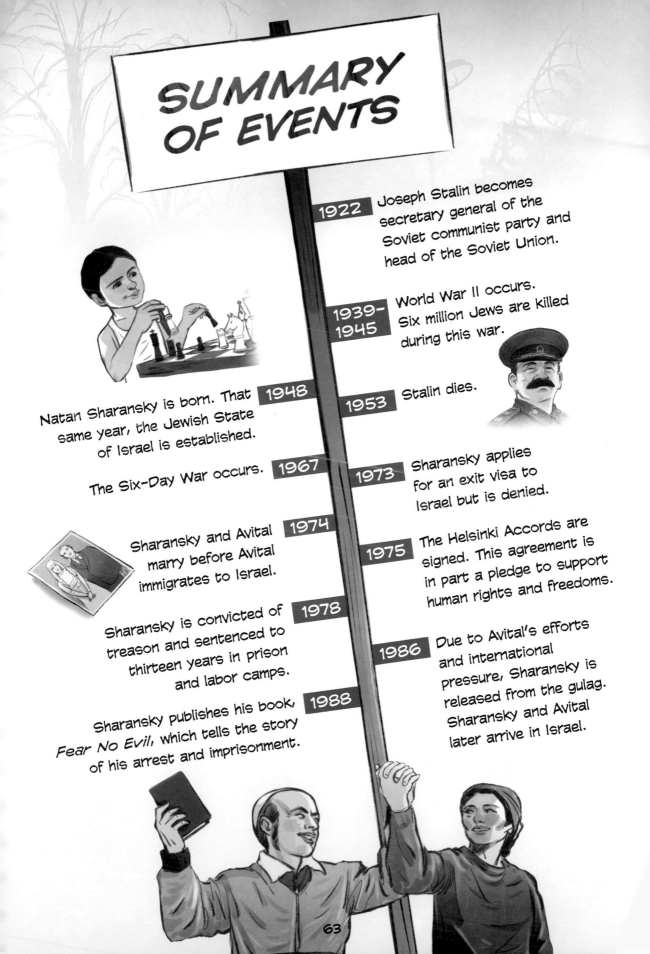

SUMMARY OF EVENTS

1922 Joseph Stalin becomes secretary general of the Soviet communist party and head of the Soviet Union.

1939–1945 World War II occurs. Six million Jews are killed during this war.

Natan Sharansky is born. That same year, the Jewish State of Israel is established. **1948**

1953 Stalin dies.

The Six-Day War occurs. **1967**

1973 Sharansky applies for an exit visa to Israel but is denied.

Sharansky and Avital marry before Avital immigrates to Israel. **1974**

1975 The Helsinki Accords are signed. This agreement is in part a pledge to support human rights and freedoms.

Sharansky is convicted of treason and sentenced to thirteen years in prison and labor camps. **1978**

1986 Due to Avital's efforts and international pressure, Sharansky is released from the gulag. Sharansky and Avital later arrive in Israel.

Sharansky publishes his book, *Fear No Evil*, which tells the story of his arrest and imprisonment. **1988**

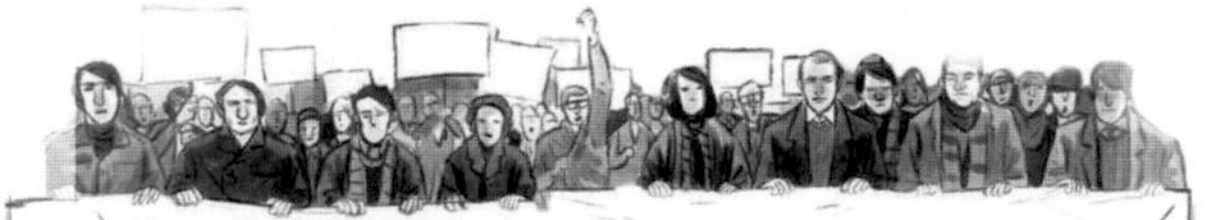

KOL YISRAEL AREVIM ZEH B'ZEH
All Israel Is Responsible Each for the Other

Natan Sharansky is a hero. He confronted a totalitarian state in his pursuit of the freedom to live his life as a Jew in the Jewish state. And he did so despite intimidation, arrest, and imprisonment.

But Natan's story is not about just one hero. The heroes of this story include his wife, his family, his friends, and Jews everywhere who answered the call of *Areyvut*: Jews helping fellow Jews in need. Thousands of Jews and others in North America, Israel, and around the world accepted the responsibility to help not just Natan, but all of Soviet Jewry, attain freedom.

Activist heroes risked arrest and imprisonment by smuggling prayer books and Jewish texts to those hungry to live Jewish lives. Activists also rallied, petitioned, and lobbied to free Soviet Jewry. Every act that helped Natan and his fellow enslaved Jews gain release was an act of heroism.

GLOSSARY

activist: a person who protests for social and political change

aliyah: immigration to Israel

anti-Semitic: relating to anti-Semitism, hostility and discrimination against Jewish people

KGB: Komitet Gosudarstvennoy Bezopasnosti, or Committee for State Security, the Soviet Union's security agency

Komsomol: a communist youth organization in the Soviet Union

Yevrei: The word *Jewish* in Russian

LEARN MORE

American Jewish Historical Society—Timeline of the American Soviet Jewry Movement
http://www.ajhs.org/timeline-american-soviet-jewry-movement

The Jewish Agency for Israel—Natan Sharansky
http://archive.jewishagency.org/executive-members/natan-sharansky

Jewish Virtual Library—Natan (Anatoly) Sharansky
https://www.jewishvirtuallibrary.org/natan-anatoly-sharansky

BIBLIOGRAPHY

Bialis, Laura, dir. *Refusenik* (2007 film). The Foundation for Documentary Projects.

Shcharansky, Anatoly. *Fear No Evil.* New York: Vintage Books, 1989.

Shcharansky, Avital and Ben-Josef, Ilana. *Next Year in Jerusalem.* New York: William Morrow and Company, 1979.